CHINA HANDBOOK SERIES

LIFE AND LIFESTYLES

Compiled by
the *China Handbook* Editorial Committee

Translated by
Chen Zhucai

FOREIGN LANGUAGES PRESS BEIJING

First Edition   1985

ISBN 0-8351-1302-7

Published by the Foreign Languages Press
24 Baiwanzhuang Road, Beijing, China

Printed by the Foreign Languages Printing House
19 West Chegongzhuang Road, Beijing, China

Distributed by the China International Book Trading
Corporation (Guoji Shudian), P.O. Box 399, Beijing, China

Printed in the People's Republic of China

More than 30 years have elapsed since the birth of the People's Republic of China on October 1, 1949. "What is China really like today?" many people abroad wish to know. To answer this question, we plan to compile and publish a voluminous *China Handbook,* in which we intend to introduce the New China in every field of its activities. Emphasis will be on the process of development during the past three decades, the accomplishments, and the problems that still remain. The book will contain accurate statistics and related materials, all of which will be ready references for an interested reader.

To enhance the usefulness of the forthcoming volume, we plan to publish 10 major sections separately at first, so that we shall have an opportunity to take into consideration the opinions of our readers before all the composite parts are put together, revised and published as one volume. These separate sections are:

Geography
History
Politics
Economy
Education and Science
Literature and the Arts
Sports and Public Health
Culture
Life and Lifestyles
Tourism

Here, we wish particularly to point out the following:

First, the statistics listed in each separate book exclude those of Taiwan, unless otherwise indicated.

Second, the statistics are those compiled up to the end of 1980 and in some cases to 1982.

The *China Handbook* Editorial Committee

CONTENTS

Chapter   One

POPULATION

1. THE PRESENT STATE OF CHINA'S POPULATION

(1) TOTAL POPULATION

China has the largest population in the world, about 22.6 per cent of the world's total. According to the *Communique of the State Statistical Bureau of the People's Republic of China Concerning the Major Statistics from the 1982 Population Census*, China's total population on July 1, 1982 was 1,031,882,511. The population of the 29 provinces, municipalities and autonomous regions on the mainland and members of the armed forces totalled 1,008,175,288 people. (Excluded from this figure was the population of Jinmen, Mazu and a few other islands of Fujian Province. The same applies to figures listed below.) The population of Taiwan Province and Jinmen, Mazu and a few other islands of Fujian Province was 18,328,596 (calculated according to figures released by Taiwan authorities). The population of Chinese compatriots in the Hong Kong and Macao regions was 5,378,627 (calculated according to figures released by Hong Kong and Macao authorities).

(2) DISTRIBUTION AND DENSITY OF THE POPULATION

The population distribution in various provinces,

municipalities, autonomous regions, and of members of the Chinese People's Liberation Army are as follows:

Distribution of the Population

Region	Population	Region	Population
Beijing	9,230,687	Guangxi Zhuang Autonomous Region	36,420,960
Tianjin	7,764,141		
Hebei Province	53,005,875	Sichuan Province	99,713,310
Shanxi Province	25,291,389		
Inner Mongolia Autonomous Region	19,274,279	Guizhou Province	28,552,997
Liaoning Province	35,721,693	Yunnan Province	32,553,817
Jilin Province	22,560,053	Tibet Autonomous Region	1,892,393
Heilongjiang Province	32,665,546	Shaanxi Province	28,904,423
Shanghai	11,859,748	Gansu Province	19,569,261
Jiangsu Province	60,521,114	Qinghai Province	3,895,706
Zhejiang Province	38,884,603	Ningxia Hui Autonomous Region	3,895,578
Anhui Province	49,665,724	Xinjiang Uygur Autonomous Region	13,081,681
Fujian Province[1]	25,931,106		
Jiangxi Province	33,184,827		
Shandong Province	74,419,054	Taiwan Province	18,270,749
Henan Province	74,422,739	Hong Kong and Macao	5,378,627
Hubei Province	47,804,150	Members of the armed forces	4,238,210
Hunan Province	54,008,851		
Guangdong Province[2]	59,299,220		

Sichuan is the province with the largest population, nearly 100 million; the Tibet Autonomous Region has the smallest, about 1.9 million.

In the total land area of 9.6 million square kilometres, the average population density per square kilometre is 107 people, an increase of 33 people over that of 74 recorded during the 1964 population census.

The population distribution is quite uneven. The population density of the 11 coastal provinces, municipalities and autonomous region increased from 232.7 people per square kilometre in 1964 to 320.6 people in 1982, an increase of 37.8 per cent. The population density of the 18 inland provinces and autonomous regions increased from 47.3 people per square kilometre to 71.4 people, a rise of 50.9 per cent. (Of these 18, the sparsely populated Tibet, Xinjiang Uygur, Ningxia Hui, Inner Mongolia autonomous regions and Qinghai and Gansu provinces increased from 7.2 people per square kilometre to 11.8 people, an increase of 63.9 per cent.)

(3) NUMBER OF HOUSEHOLDS

In the 29 provinces, municipalities and autonomous regions on the mainland, there are a total of 1,073,010 collective households (consisting of living quarters for single men or women of enterprises, schools, and government organizations and other institutions), with a population

---

[1] The population of Fujian Province included that of 57,847 of Jinmen, Mazu and a few other islands.

[2] In the population of Guangdong Province, the figures for the Dongsha Islands and Nansha Islands were not included.

of 32,952,506; and 220,100,775 family households, with a population of 970,984,572. Family households average 4.41 people.

2. POPULATION COMPOSITION

(1) SEX COMPOSITION

On July 1, 1982, the male population of the 29 provinces, municipalities and autonomous regions and members of the armed forces numbered 519,433,369, accounting for 51.5 per cent of the total population, and females numbered 488,741,919, accounting for 48.5 per cent, the proportion of males to females being 106.3 to 100.

In old China, the proportion of males was high. According to the census data of the reign of Xuantong (1909-1911) of the Qing Dynasty, compiled in 1912, males numbered 202,038,866 and females 166,107,654, the proportion of males to females being 121.6 to 100. According to the census of 1932 to 1939, the proportion of males to females was 112.17 to 100. According to New China's first national census of 1953, the proportion of males to females was 107.6 to 100, a clear decrease from that of the old China. At the second national census of 1964, the proportion of males to females further decreased to 105.5 to 100.

(2) AGE COMPOSITION

According to the 1953 and 1964 census figures of the various provinces, municipalities and autonomous regions on the mainland and the 1982 census figures of three provinces, the percentages of children, old people and those between 15 and 64 in the total population were as follows:

Age Composition of the Population

Census Year	Age Group	Provinces, Municipalities and Autonomous Regions on the Mainland	Average of Hebei, Henan and Zhejiang Provinces	Hebei Province	Henan Province	Zhejiang Province
1953	14 and under	36.28	35.70	35.98	35.71	35.24
	15-64	59.31	59.01	57.78	59.16	60.68
	65 and over	4.41	5.29	6.24	5.13	4.08
1964	14 and under	40.41	40.53	40.96	39.75	41.23
	15-64	55.72	55.00	54.25	55.94	54.55
	65 and over	3.87	4.47	4.79	4.31	4.22
1982	14 and under	Not yet available	32.28	30.78	34.90	29.30
	15-64		62.23	63.55	59.88	64.95
	65 and over		5.49	5.67	5.22	5.75

It can be seen from the above table that: 1) Children 14 years old and under make up about 32 per cent of the total population. Owing to a decrease in birthrates during the 1970s, China's population of 15-year-olds and under is relatively small in comparison with other developing countries, which have populations in this category of about 39 per cent. 2) The percentage of the population of people between 15 and 64 has increased greatly. 3) The percentage of the population of old people is fairly small, as people 65 and over reached only 5 per cent plus. The data above shows that China's age composition at present has changed gradually from a growing type in 1964 to a stable type now.

(3) NATIONALITIES COMPOSITION

On July 1, 1982, the population of the Han nationality in the 29 provinces, municipalities and autonomous regions was 936.7 million, accounting for 93.3 per cent of the total; the minority nationalities population was 67.23 million, making up 6.7 per cent.

Compared with the 1964 census figures, the Han nationality population increased by 285.41 million, or 43.8 per cent, and the minority nationalities population increased by 27.31 million, or 68.4 per cent. The percentage of the latter population in the total rose from 5.8 per cent in 1964 to 6.7 per cent in 1982. This was mainly because the Chinese government put into effect a correct nationalities policy and regional national autonomy, giving minority nationalities great support in their economic and cultural development. At the same time, the state was rather generous towards the minority nationalities in the matter of family planning. Some nationalities with small populations increased more rapidly. For example, the Qiang nationality, living in Sichuan Province, increased from 49,105 people in 1964 to 102,768 in 1982, a rise of 109.3 per cent. And the Hezhen nationality, living in Heilongjiang Province, increased from 718 people in 1964 to 1,476 in 1982, a growth of 105.6 per cent.

Of the 55 minority nationalities in the 29 provinces, municipalities and autonomous regions, 15 have populations of over one million each, namely, the Zhuang, Hui, Uygur, Yi, Miao, Manchu, Tibetan, Mongolian, Tujia, Bouyei, Korean, Dong, Yao, Bai and Hani. Thirteen have populations of over 100,000 each: the Kazak, Dai, Li, Lisu, She, Lahu, Va, Shui, Dongxiang, Naxi, Tu, Kirgiz and Qiang. Seven have populations of over 50,000 each: the Daur, Jingpo, Mulam, Xibe, Salar, Blang and Gelo. Twenty have populations of under 50,000 each: the Maonan, Tajik, Pumi, Nu, Achang, Ewneki, Jino, Ozbek, Jing, Benglong, Yugur, Bonan, Moinba, Drung, Oroqen, Tatar, Russian, Lhoba, Gaoshan and Hezhen.

(4) EDUCATION LEVEL COMPOSITION

On July 1, 1982, over 4.41 million persons among the population of the 29 provinces, municipalities and autonomous regions were university graduates, and 1.6 million others had attended universities (including both those who studied but did not finish and those then attending university). Persons with a senior middle school education numbered more than 66.47 million, and there were 178.27 million people who had attained the junior middle school level. There were 355.16 million people with a primary school education.

Compared with 1964, those with university educations had increased by 3.14 million in the 18 years up to 1982; those with senior middle school educations had increased by 57.36 million; those with junior middle school educations had increased by 145.93 million; and those with primary school educations had increased by 159.33 million.

Before Liberation, over 80 per cent of China's population was illiterate. After the founding of New China, 40 million people had become literate by 1958. Compared with the 1964 census figures, the percentage of illiterates and semi-illiterates in the total population dropped from 38.1 per cent to 23.5 per cent by the 1982 census. But progress in the elimination of illiteracy is still not rapid enough.

(5) COMPOSITION OF WORKING POPULATION IN TERMS OF BRANCHES OF WORK

In the 30 and more years since Liberation, China's working popoulation has been increasing steadily, and the proportion in relationship to the total population has been rising too.

At the end of 1981, the working population in the 29 provinces, municipalities and autonomous regions numbered 432.8 million, accounting for 43.4 per cent of the total population. Of this number, 83.72 million, or 19.3 per cent, were workers and staff members of units of ownership by the whole people; 25.68 million, or 5.9 per cent, were members of units of collective ownership in cities and towns; 1.13 million, or 0.3 per cent, were people working on their own in cities and towns; and 322.27 million, or 74.5 per cent, were collective and individual agricultural workers.

The composition of the working population in terms of branches of work at the end of 1981 is as follows:

Composition of the Working Population

	Number of Work Force (In 10,000 persons)	%
Total	43,280	100
Industry	5,796	13.4
Building Industry, Natural Resources Prospecting	1,274	2.9
Agriculture, Forestry, Water Conservancy, Meteorology	31,171	72.0
Transport, Post and Telecommunications	833	1.9
Commerce, Food and Drink, Service Trades, Materials Supply	1,722	4.0
Scientific Research, Culture, Education, Public Health, Social Welfare	1,645	3.8
Government and Mass organizations	555	1.3
Others	284	0.7

(6) URBAN AND RURAL COMPOSITION

On July 1, 1982, the total population inhabiting the cities (not including counties under the direct administration of cities) and towns of the 29 provinces, municipalities and autonomous regions was 206,588,582. The total population of the 236 cities was 144,679,340, and that of the 2,664 towns was 61,909,242.

Compared with the 1964 census figures, the population of the cities and towns had increased by 79,485,541 people, or 62.5 percent, a higher rate than that of the 45.1 per cent increase for China's total population. During the 18 years, the percentage of the population of the cities and towns in the country's total had grown from 18.4 per cent of 1964 to 20.6 per cent, a rise of slightly more than one tenth.

3. GENERAL SURVEY OF POPULATION DEVELOPMENT

(1) POPULATION OF THE SUCCESSIVE DYNASTIES

China was one of the first countries in the world to calculate its population. Her most ancient extant population figure was that of 13.55 million in the Xia Dynasty of the 21st century B.C. In the 11th century B.C., the population of the Western Zhou Dynasty was recorded as 13.71 million. In this period of slave society, owing to low productivity and incessant warfare, China's total population stayed at around 10 million.

During the period of feudal society, China's population increased fairly rapidly, reaching 59.59 million in the second year of the reign of Yuanshi of Emperor Pingdi of the Western Han Dynasty (A.D. 2). Thereafter, because of wars and natural disasters, and the fact that governments of the successive Han, Tang, Song, Ming and other dynasties levied a poll tax, the population fluctuated between 50 million and 60 million, and sometimes fell even lower. During the reign of Qianlong of the Qing Dynasty, a land tax instead of a poll tax was levied. The population figure increased quite rapidly after that because there were fewer concealments of the real number of family members. The population increased from more than 140 million in the sixth year of the reign of Qianlong (1741) to more than 410 million in the 21st year of the reign of Daoguang (1841).

In modern times, China's population of more than 410 million during the Opium War of 1840 increased to more than 541 million at the end of 1949 when China was liberated. During these 109 years, the population increased by more than 120 million, at an average annual growth rate of 2.5 per thousand.

Despite the fact that there are legitimate reasons to doubt the accuracy of these ancient population figures and the fact that the territories of the various dynasties differed and the objects of the censuses were not uniform (some counted in terms of households, some in terms of able-bodied men, etc.), it is still possible to use them to gain a general view of China's population through the successive dynasties.

China's Population of the Successive Dynasties

	Period of Reign	Year	Population	Source
Xia	Xia Dynasty	c. 2100 B.C.	13,553,923	Di Wang Shi Ji (Biographies of Emperors)
Zhou	King Cheng	c. 1100 B.C.	13,714,923	Di Wang Shi Ji (Biographies of Emperors)
Han	2nd year of the Yuanshi reign of Emperor Pingdi of the Western Han	A.D. 2	59,594,978	Han Shu (History of the Han Dynasty), "Chapter on Geography"
	2nd year of the Zhongyuan reign of Emperor Guangwu of the Eastern Han	57	21,007,820	Hou Han Shu (History of the Later Han Dynasty), "Chapter on Prefectures and Principalities"
	3rd year of the Yongshou reign of Emperor Huandi of the Eastern Han	157	56,486,850	Tong Dian (Encyclopedia of Rules and Systems), "Chapter on Economic History"
	Three Kingdoms (Shu, Wei and Wu)	263	7,672,881	Tong Dian (Encyclopedia of Rules and Systems), "Chapter on Economic History"

China's Population of the Successive Dynasties (continued)

	Period of Reign	Year	Population	Source
Jin	1st year of the Taikang reign of Emperor Wu-di of the Western Jin	280	16,163,863	*Jin Shu History of the Jin Dynasty),* "Chapter on Geography"
Sui	5th year of the Daye reign of Emperor Yangdi	609	46,019,956	*Sui Shu (History of the Sui Dynasty),* "Chapter on Geography"
Tang	14th year of the Tian-bao reign of Emperor Xuanzong	755	52,919,309	*Tong Dian (Encyclopedia of Rules and Systems),* "Chapter on Economic History"
Song	4th year of the Daguan reign of Emperor Hui-zong	1110	46,734,784	*Song Shi (History of the Song Dynasty),* "Chapter on Geography"
Yuan	28th year of the Zhi-yuan reign of Emperor Shizu	1291	59,848,964	*Yuan Shi (History of the Yuan Dynasty),* Vol. 16, "Basic Annals of Emperor Shizu"

China's Population of the Successive Dynasties (continued)

	Period of Reign	Year	Population	Source
Ming	22nd year of the Cheng-hua reign of Emperor Xianzong	1486	65,442,600	Ming Shi Lu (Veritable Records of the Ming Dynasty), "Veritable Records of the Chenghua Reign of Emperor Xianzong"
Qing	6th year of the Qianlong reign of Emperor Gaozong	1741	143,411,559	Qing Shi Lu (Veritable Records of the Qing Dynasty), "Emperor Gaozong", Vol. 157
	24th year of the Jiaqing reign of Emperor Renzong	1819	301,260,545	Dong Hua Xu Lu (Sequel of Donghua Records) by Wang Xianqian
	21st year of the Daoguang reign of Emperor Xuanzong	1841	413,457,311	Qing Shi Lu (Veritable Records of the Qing Dynasty), "Emperor Xuanzong", Vol. 364.
Republic of China	20th year of the Republic	1931	475,000,000	Shen Bao Nian Jian (Shen Bao Yearbook)

(2) POPULATION GROWTH OF NEW CHINA

In the first 20 years after the founding of New China, owing to insufficient understanding of the importance of limiting population growth, China was unable to control her population growth in a planned way. Thus the number of people increased rapidly. During the early 70s, she began to carry out a policy of planned birth control and the growth rate has since dropped year by year. In the 32 years after Liberation, China's total population increased by 466.5 million persons, averaging an annual increase of 14.35 million, or an average annual growth rate of 1.9 per cent. However, population growth over the years showed variations, which can roughly be divided into four stages: two baby booms, one recession and one decline.

1) From the beginning of 1950 to the end of 1957 was the period of the first baby boom. The population increased from 541.67 million to 646.53 million, averaging an annual increase of 13.11 million, or an average annual growth rate of 2.2 per cent.

2) From the beginning of 1958 to the end of 1961 was the period of recession in population growth. The population increased from 646.53 million to 658.59 million, averaging an annual increase of 3.02 million, or an average annual growth rate of only 0.5 per cent.

3) From the beginning of 1962 to the end of 1973 was the period of the second baby boom. The population increased from 658.59 million to 891.43 million, averaging an annual increase of 19.4 million, or an average annual growth rate of 2.6 per cent.

4) From the beginning of 1974 to July 1, 1982 was the period of population decline. The population increased

from 891.43 million to 1,008.17 million, averaging an annual increase of 13.73 million, or an average annual growth rate of 1.5 per cent.

The rapid population growth in New China was mainly due to the following causes:

1) Large Decline of Mortality Rates. People's improved livelihood, rapid development of medical and health services and step-by-step control of epidemic diseases brought about a large decline of mortality rates. Before Liberation, China's mortality rate was about 25 per thousand. According to an investigation of some areas in 1952, the average mortality rate was then 17 per thousand. This dropped to 9.6 per thousand in 1965 and to 6.36 per thousand in 1981.

Owing to the decline of mortality rates and improved nutrition and better health, average life expectancy has been greatly lengthened. The average life span in old China was around 35 years. This increased to 57 in 1957 and to 69 in 1980, registering nearly a twofold rise.

2) Relatively High Birthrates. Before 1971, the birthrate in China was basically not controlled. Thus, during the more than 20 years after 1949, the average birthrate remained around 35 per thousand. In the early 70s, owing to conscientious implementation of family planning, birthrates dropped from around 35 per thousand to around 20 per thousand. Natural growth rates also dropped from around 25 per thousand to around 15 per thousand. In 1981, the birthrate was 20.91 per thousand and the natural growth rate was 14.55 per thousand. At present, the downward trend of birthrates is continuing.

The fact that China's birthrates stayed at a relatively high level in the first 20 years and more after the founding of New China can be attributed to several causes.

Firstly, China's economy is relatively backward, which is even more evident in the countryside where the main form of labour is still manual. The income of a peasant family basically is determined by the number of its members engaged in labour and by their physical strength. Moreover, it is still difficult for the state and the collective to provide social insurance for old people in the countryside on a large scale, so that many peasants cherish the idea of begetting more children so as to increases family income through labour and on whom they can depend in old age. These are the economic reasons for peasants to want more children, especially boys. In addition, there are the traditional ideas that have evolved over more than 2,000 years of Chinese feudal society, such as the ideas of "the more sons, the more blessings" and "of the three unfilial acts, to have no son is the worst". These have exerted a deep influence on the peasant masses, so that the old custom of early marriage and many births is still prevalent in the countryside.

Besides, there was much one-sidedness in the propaganda relating to population theory in China. After Liberation, with the termination of the long years of war and the carrying out of land reform, the peasant masses were allotted land for the first time. Many of them immediately married and had children. Early in the 50s, China's too rapid population growth caused concern among some sociologists and economists. Ma Yinchu, a noted economist who was then President of Beijing University, published an article entitled "New Population Theory". He advocated a vigorous control of population size and improvement of population quality. But his correct theory and proposition were not adopted. In the propaganda relating to population theory, the aspect of

man as producer was one-sidely stressed. This was also
a reason why birthrates failed to decline over a long
period of time.

Furthermore, the fact that the many people lacked
knowledge of the physiological process of conception because their scientific and educational level was not high,
and the fact that scientific contraception had not yet been
well popularized, also affected voluntary birth control.

Thus China's population growth changed from the
high birthrates, high mortality rates and low growth rates
of old China to high birthrates, low mortality rates and
high growth rates in the first 20 years after the founding
of New China. At present, China's population is changing
towards the stage of low birthrates, low mortality rates
and low growth rates.

4. POPULATION CONTROL AND FAMILY PLANNING

(1) POPULATION CONTROL TARGET

For the purpose of accelerating socialist modernization, China's general objective in economic construction
is: to increase the gross value of industrial and agricultural production from 710 billion yuan in 1980 to 2,800
billion yuan or so in 2000. At the same time, utmost
efforts must be given to keeping the population within
1.2 billion. If this population control target is attained,
the gross value of industrial and agricultural production
per capita will increase from 719.6 yuan in 1980 to 2,333.3
yuan, an increase of 3.24 times. The income of the urban
and rural population will then increase several times over,

and the Chinese people will be comparatively well-off both materially and culturally.

As required by the population control target mentioned above, the population increase during the 18 and a half years until the end of this century must be kept under 191.82 million, averaging an annual natural increase of 10.37 million. After taking into account deductions caused by annual mortality, we can see that the number of annual births must be kept between 16 million and 17 million, with the annual birthrates gradually dropping to below 16 per thousand. In other words, they must drop nearly one-fourth from the present birthrate of more than 20 per thousand. China's present situation is one in which there is a great population base number and an especially large proportion of young people, with the population of 21-year-olds and under making up 50 per cent, or 500 million. Moreover, China's population at present is in the period of a baby boom, which is expected to continue for more than 10 years. However, if population growth is strictly and effectively controlled and the policy of only one child per couple is widely propagated and resolutely implemented among the annual 12 million newly married couples of child-bearing age, then it is possible to attain the target of keeping the population within 1.2 billion by the end of this century. China's most populous Sichuan Province has already succeeded in lowering its birthrate from 37.16 per thousand in 1972 to 17.96 per thousand in 1981.

(2) FAMILY PLANNING MEASURES

Family planning is an important component part of China's population policy. The 12th National Congress of the Communist Party of China has affirmed that family planning is a basic national policy. This is an important strategic decision made after summing up the experiences and lessons gained from China's population problem in the 30 and more years since the founding of New China. Article 25 of the Constitution of the People's Republic of China stipulates: "The state promotes family planning so that population growth may fit the plan for economic and social development." The basic requirements of family planning are: late marriage, late childbirth, few births and better babies.

Late Marriage and Late Childbirth. Article 5 of the new Marriage Law states: "Late marriage and late childbirth should be encouraged" and sets the lawful marriageable age at 22 years for man and 20 years for women. Generally speaking, a marriage that has been postponed for three years or more from the lawful age is a late marriage; a woman giving birth at 24 years of age or above is considered to be engaging in late childbirth. The advocacy of suitably late marriage and late childbirth for young people has great significance in adjusting baby booms and in lowering population growth. If young women begin childbirth at 20 years of age, five generations will be produced in 100 years; if they begin childbirth at 25 years of age, only four generations will be produced in 100 years. Late marriage and late childbirth are also of benefit to young people in their study and work, and in their family welfare.

Few Births. "Few births" means implementing the policy of only one child per couple. In the case of certain couples who have experienced difficulties — whose first child, for example, was disabled by illness and cannot grow up to be a normal worker — a second child is permitted. As for those couples of reproductive age who already have two children, they are generally persuaded to adopt birth control measures that are permanent, safe and beneficial to their health so as to prevent a third birth. In the case of the minority nationalities, family planning is also advocated, with a suitable relaxation in the requirements.

Better Babies. The purpose of family planning is not only to control the population numerically, but to raise its quality. The first step is one of guaranteeing that babies are healthy and intelligent so that children will be born well and grow up strong and useful. In order to avoid the birth of mentally deficient children or children with hereditary diseases, due to marriage of near relations or people with hereditary diseases, the Chinese Government has established some legal provisions. Many hospitals and family planning instruction centres have set up outpatient consultation services to deal with marriage problems, production of better babies, and hereditary diseases. Thus they provide eugenic guidance for young men and women. At the same time, maternity and child health care services have been strengthened so as to improve the work of maternity and child health care during pregnancy and childbirth, feeding babies and infants, and early education.

In controlling population growth and carrying out family planning, the Chinese government has adopted the following concrete measures:

1) **Formulating Population Plans.** Since the early 70s, China has included population reproduction in the orbit of planning, co-ordinating this with material production. In drawing up five-year plans and annual plans, the government has considered not only development of

material production but also population growth, outlining
plans for the number of births down to the level of communes, production brigades, factories, mines and other
enterprises, and even individuals.

2) **Carrying Out Propaganda for Education on Family Planning.** Through the mass media — radio, tele-
vision, the press, films, etc. — the Chinese government has
conducted propaganda among the people about the importance of family planning and has explained the advan-
tages of controlling population growth in realizing the
four modernizations, developing the collective economy,
improving family life and emancipating women. The
propoganda also aims constantly at exploding such feudal
ideas as "men are honourable and women lowly" and "the
more sons, the more blessings." The propaganda is also
directed toward the protection of female babies and the
protection of women who have given birth to them from
discrimination. In this way it has made family planning
a general concept of society and part of the conscious actions of the masses. In some areas, propaganda and
education have been carried out in a deep-going way so
that general knowledge of population theory, family planning and eugenics has been popularized. Between New
Year and the Spring Festival of 1983, nationwide activities to mark Family Planning Propaganda Month brought
a new upsurge in education on family planning.

3) **Implementing the Responsibility System in Family Planning and Adopting Necessary Economic Measures.** The Sixth Five-Year Plan of the People's Republic
of China for Economic and Social Development stipulates: "While implementing various forms of the production
responsibility system, the rural areas must also establish
a corresponding responsibility system for family plan-

ning." At present, many rural areas practise the system of communes and production brigades signing family planning contracts with married couples of childbearing age. Cadres in charge of family planning rely on the system of personal responsibility and the system of signing technical responsibility contracts with such medical departments as commune hospitals in carrying out their work.

Ideological education has mainly been relied on in promoting family planning, while people's governments in all parts of China have laid down socio-economic measures favourable to family planning. These measures put into effect the principle of both rewards and penalties, with stress on the former. Couples who give birth to only one child are commended and rewarded. Preferential treatment is given to only children and their families in such matters as admission into nurseries and schools, medical treatment, worker recruitment, enrolment of new students, and allocation of housing space in urban centres and housing land in rural areas.

4) **Strengthening Technical Guidance in Birth Control.** Contraception is the principal method of birth control, and China advocates comprehensive contraceptive measures. Under the guidance of medical personnel, couples of reproductive age can choose the kind of contraception to use according to their physical conditions. Only after contraception fails, owing to carelessness, is induced abortion applied.

To lighten the economic burden on the masses, the state supplies contraceptives and provides induced abortion or surgical sterilization free of charge. It stipulates that definite periods of leave with full pay are granted according to different surgical operations undergone.

Some factories, mines and other enterprises and some communes and production brigades stipulate that those who have undergone such operations shall be issued nutrition allowances and given preferential treatment in their daily life.

5) **Setting Up Family Planning Agencies.** In 1971, the Family Planning Office of the State Council was established. Later, family planning agencies of the local governments at various levels were formed step by step. In 1981, the State Family Planning Commission was established. In China, people's communes, factories, government organizations and other institutions, schools and neighbourhood organizations all have full-time or part-time family planning personnel. They carry out propaganda among the masses, help couples of reproductive age make childbearing plans, and make intensive investigations so as to provide the basis for state decisions on population policy.

6) **Intensifying Research in Population Theory.** In 1979, the Ministry of Education of the Chinese government decided to establish a system of demographic teaching and research in the institutions of higher learning. The Institute of Economics of the Chinese Academy of Social Sciences has also engaged in population research and is now preparing to establish a population research centre. In recent years, the academies of social sciences in the various provinces, municipalities and autonomous regions have also set up population research institutes, one after another. In February 1981, the China Demographic Society was founded. Between 1978 and 1981, three national demographic symposia were held, at which research results were exchanged and valuable proposals submitted to the government.

Chapter Two

MINORITY NATIONALITIES

1. GENERAL INFORMATION

(1) POPULATION

On the vast expanse of China's richly endowed land live 56 different ethnic groups with a total population of more than 1,031,000,000.

The Han nationality is the largest, not only in China but also in the world. With 936,700,000 people, the Hans make up approximately 93.3 per cent of China's population. Mostly concentrated in the Huanghe, Changjiang and Zhujiang river valleys and on the Songhualiaohe Plains of northeast China, the Hans play a leading role in the life of the country.

Apart from the Han nationality the other 55 ethnic groups, with a total of more than 67.23 million people, constitute roughly 6.7 per cent of China's population. But there is a great difference in the size of population of these various minority nationalities:

Nationalities with populations of over one million are: the Zhuang, Hui, Uygur, Yi, Miao, Manchu, Tibetan, Mongolian, Tujia, Bouyei, Korean, Dong, Yao, Bai and Hani. The largest of these is the Zhuang, with more than 13 million.

Those with populations of between one million and 100,000 are the Kazak, Dai, Li, Lisu, She, Lahu, Va, Shui, Dongxiang, Naxi, Tu, Kirgiz and Qiang. Those with populations of between 100,000 and 50,000 are: the Daur, Jingpo, Mulam, Xibe, Salar, Blang and Gelo. And there are 20 nationalities each with less than 50,000. These are the Maonan, Tajik, Pumi, Nu, Achang, Ewenki, Jino, Ozbek, Jing, Benglong, Yugur, Bonan, Moinba, Drung, Oroqen, Tatar, Russian, Lhoba, Gaoshan (in Taiwan) and Hezhen.

(2) DISTRIBUTION

Although small in size, the peoples of the various minority nationalities live over a very wide area constituting 50 to 60 per cent of the country. This area includes Inner Mongolia, Xinjiang, Tibet, Guangxi, Ningxia, Heilongjiang, Jilin, Liaoning, Gansu, Qinghai, Sichuan, Yunnan, Guizhou, Guangdong, Hunan, Hebei, Hubei, Fujian and Taiwan.

The places where the minority nationalities live have the following common characteristics.

1) A wide expanse of land with a sparse distribution of population. Though the whole area of national autonomous regions, prefectures, counties and districts totals 6,106,000 square kilometres, or 63.63 per cent of the land, only about 109.085 million people, that is, only 11.19 per cent of China's whole population, live in these regions. And of this number, only 43.5 million are of the minority nationalities. This is 39.81 per cent of the whole population in these places. Many minority nationalities have traditionally established their abodes in mountainous and pastoral areas, on high plateaus and in deep forests.

2) A wide range of products and abundant mineral resources. The agricultural crops grown on the vast expanses of fertile land in the areas of the minority nationalities constitute a wide variety. The areas are rich in cotton, sugar cane, rubber, coffee and many varieties of melons and fruits. The areas also contain the country's five natural grazing grounds, abounding in sheep, goats, horses, cattle, camels and yaks. In addition, they contain a great wealth of water resources, many dense forests and abundant mineral resources. Surveys show that the mineral deposits are large in variety and quantity. For example, iron is found at Baiyunebo in Inner Mongolia, oil at Yumen in Gansu and Karamay in Xinjiang, boron and copper in Tibet, gold in the Altay Mountains of Xinjiang and jade at Hotan.

Principal Natural Resources of the National Autonomous Areas and Their Percentage in Relation to the Whole Country
(According to 1980 Statistics)

	1980 Absolute Figures	Percentage
Area under cultivation	16,600,000 hectares	16.7
Steppe land	286,000,000 hectares	89.6
Of which, the usable area	223,330,000 hectares	99.5
Forested area	45,330,000 hectares	37.8

Accumulation of wood	4,300 million cubic metres	46
Hydraulic reserve	353,340,000 kw.	52.3

3) Strategic importance as border regions for the whole country. China has a border line of more than 20,000 kilometres, adjoining 12 countries. Great contributions have been made by people of various minority nationalities, who live in the 136 counties adjoining the border, together with people of the Han nationality to the country's national defence and construction.

The vissititudes of the time, immigration and reclamation throughout history has led to many shifts of population in the border areas. Thus people of different nationalities today live together in the various minority nationality areas.

History shows that the Han people were already widely distributed over the country in early times. Today, they not only live in great numbers in the communities largely populated by people of one or another minority nationality, but in many minority areas the Hans constitute the majority of the population. At the same time, in the areas of the Han people there are usually found small communities of people from one or more of the minority nationalities. Incomplete statistics show that over 70 per cent of counties and cities in China today have a permanent presence of people of more than two nationalities.

Intermingling between the various minority nationalities is also seen. Take the Xinjiang Uygur Autonomous

Region, for example. In this region there are altogether 13 different nationalities, including the Uygur, Han, Kazak, Hui, Kirgiz, Mongolian, Russian, Tajik, Ozbek, Xibe, Tatar, Daur and Manchu. In the Guangxi Zhuang Autonomous Region there are the Yao, Miao, Dong, Mulam, Maonan, Hui, Jing, Yi, Shui and Gelo, in addition to the Zhuang and Han nationalities.

For a long time some of these minority nationalities have existed in a number of different national communities throughout the country. Take the Tibetan nationality, for example. In early post-liberation days it had a total population of some 2,700,000 people, but only 1,200,000 of these lived in Tibet. The greater number of Tibetans lived in Qinghai, Gansu, Sichuan and Yunnan.

Although they generally live together with people of the Han nationality, the minority nationalities have always had their own communities. Yet with the mutual influence on each other in the fields of economy, politics and culture, they have also formed close ties with the Han people.

(3) SPOKEN AND WRITTEN LANGUAGES

Among the 55 minority nationalities of China only the Hui and Manchu nationalities use the language of the Hans. The others speak their own languages. A total of 29 have languages in the Han-Tibetan language family. These groups are distributed in central south and southwest China. There are 17 with languages in the Altaic language family. These are found in northeast and northwest China. Five have languages in the language family

of South Asia, and two have languages in the Indo-European language family. In the Nandao language family
there is the Gaoshan nationality, and there is one nationality whose language origin has not yet been identified.

The following table shows the language families of
the 55 minority nationalities. (See pp. 31 & 32)

Before Liberation there were 21 minority nationalities
that had their own written languages. Among these there
were only 11 (Mongolian, Tibetan, Uygur, Korean, Kazak,
Xibo, Dai, Ozbek, Kirgiz, Tatar and Russian) that had
commonly used written scripts. Seven (Yi, Naxi, Miao,
Jingpo, Suli, Lahu and Va) had their own written scripts,
but these were not commonly used; and three nationalities (Hui, Manchu and She) used the written script of the
Hans. Some of these written languages were pictographic
or ideographic scripts, others had alphabets or syllabic
systems. The latter were written in Tibetan, Korean,
Uygur, Dai, Arabic, Latin or Slavic symbols. There were
also some minority nationalities that used several written
scripts concurrently. The Dai nationality, for example,
had four, while the Mongolians had two.

After Liberation, the people's government, in the
process of facilitating the progress of various nationalities, assisted the Zhuang, Bouyei, Miao, Yi, Dong, Hani,
Suli, Va, Li and Naxi in either standerdizing their written scripts or developing new ones. And five nationalities — the Uygur, Kazak, Jingpo, Lahu and Dai — reformed their written scripts.

(4) UNEVEN DEVELOPMENT BEFORE LIBERATION

Before Liberation the social and economic development of the various nationalites was most uneven. Gen-

Language Families of the Minority Nationalities

The Han-Tibetan language family —

— Zhuang-Dong
language group: Zhuang, Bouyei, Dai, Dong, Mulam, Shui, Maonan and Li.

— Tibeto-Burman
language group: Tibetan, Moinba, Yi, Lisu, Naxi, Hani, Lahu, Jino, Jingpo, Drung, Qiang and Pumi.

Language branch to be further identified: Lhoba, Nu, Achang and Bai.

— Miao-Yao
language group: Miao, She and Yao.

— Language group and branch to be further identified: Tujia and Mulam.

— Han language
group: Hui and Manchu.

The Altaic language family —

— Turkic language
group: Uygur, Salar, Ozbek, Kazak, Tatar, Yugur and Kirgiz.

— Mongolian language group: Mongolian, Tu, Dongxiang, Daur, Bonan and Yugur.

— Manchu Tungusic
language group: Manchu, Xibo, Zezhen, Oroqen and Ewenki.

— Language group branch
to be further identified: Korean.

The South Asian language family — Va, Benglong and Blang.

The Malayo-Polynesian language family — Gaoshan.

The Indo European language family —
- —Slavic language group: Russian.
- —Iranian language group: Tajik.

Language family, group and branch to be further identified: — Jing.

erally speaking, the social and economic development of
the Han people was on a higher plane than that for most of
the minority nationalities. The Hans had a well-developed
feudal agricultural economy, with elements of capitalism
developing within it. Wherever the minority nationalities
lived in close proximity to communities of the Han people, their social economy had much the same features.
But for the minority nationalities that lived far from the
Han people, their social economy remained in a quite
backward state. Some had an economy based on primitive
fishing and hunting, others on a pastoral life, and still
others practised slash and burn agriculture. The economic
systems in these areas of minority nationalities before
Liberation ranged from those with some vestiges of primitive communalism through slave to feudal serf systems.

There were then more than 30 minorities that had
social and economic structures that were largely identical
with those of the Hans. These included the Zhuang, Hui,
Uygur, Korean, Manchu, Bouyei, Bai, Tujia, Dong and
Miao nationalities, as well as most of the Mongolians, Yis
and Lis and a few Tibetans, altogether about 30 million
of people. In the areas of these minority nationalities the
two main classes were composed of landlords and peasants. To varying degrees elements of capitalism had even
developed among 20 of these nationalities, including the
Huis, Manchus, Uygurs, Zhuangs, Bouyeis and Koreans.

The minority nationalities that still lived under a
feudal serf system were the Tibetans, Dais and Hanis,
altogether about four million people. Feudal lords and
serfs made up the two main classes for these groups. The
hereditary serfs were subjected to all kinds of exploitation in terms of rent, usury and corvées. In some parts of
Inner Mongolia there was some feudal pastoral serfdom.

At the time of Liberation in the Greater and Lesser Liangshan Mountains of Sichuan and Yunnan provinces slavery was practised among the one million people of the Yi nationality. Black Yis (nobles), who comprised about 7 per cent of the Yi population, owned over 70 per cent of the land and most of the draught animals. The slaves, whom the slaveowners had completely in their power, were subjected to ruthless oppression.

There were also some minority nationalities at the time of Liberation who subsisted under varying degrees of primitive communalism. Among these were the Drung, Nu, Suli, Jingpo, Va and Blang nationalities, living in the mountainous border areas of Yunnan; the Oroqen and Ewenki nationalities, living in Inner Mongolia; some of the Yi people in the Wuzhi Mountains on Hainan Island, and some of the Gaoshan people living in Taiwan — altogether about 0.6 million of people. Although these minority nationalities had begun to develop individual production and divide into classes, vestiges of primitive communalism remained, with the means of production being publicly owned, production being collectively carried out, and fruits of labour being equally distributed.

Following Liberation, the government, in accordance with a cautious policy of making steady progress while taking into account the specific characteristics of the various minority nationalities, enabled one nationality after another to adopt the socialist road. Using the new Land Reform Law, the government saw to it that where their social and economic structures were the same as that of the Hans, land reforms were carried out in ways similar to those of the Hans, and measures were taken to gradually move them toward socialist agricultural cooperation.

In areas where the minority nationalities still practised feudal serfdom, reforms were carried out through "peaceful consultation" in line with a policy of redemption towards elements of the upper classes. Feudal serfdom was thus ended among the Dai and Hani peoples. But in feudal areas inhabited by the Tibetan and Yi people a number of reactionary members of the upper classes took the path of armed rebellion. It was only after the suppression of these revolts that the obsolete serf and slave system were ended.

In the areas where there were still vestiges of primitive communalism and there was no sharp class distinction, no reforms were carried out. Efforts, however, were made to develop the economy and culture in these areas so as to bring about a gradual democratic transformation. In 1959 the peoples of these areas took the socialist road, transcending several historical stages of development.

2. A COUNTRY, UNITED AND OF MANY NATIONALITIES

China has always been a country of many nationalities. In the long course of historical development and in creating the great culture of the Chinese nation, these nationalities have combined themselves into a great people.

(1) MAKING A COMMON EFFORT TO BUILD A UNITED COUNTRY

United and multi-national, China is a country coming into being as a collective creation of the whole Chinese

people.   From time immemorial our forefathers laboured,
lived and multiplied on this land.   The earliest histories
say that the people living on the Central Plains in the
Huanghe River valley were those called the Xia.   In the
area from the Huaihe River to Mount Taishan in the
eastern part of the country were those called the Dongyi;
in the Changjiang River valley in the south were those
called the Sanmiao; in the area beyond the Huanghe River
in the northwest were those called the Qiang; and in the
area to the south and north of the deserts in the north of
the country were those called the Hunzhou.   The Xia
people established various links with the people of other
nationalities living in their vicinity.   From the Shang
and Western Zhou dynasties to the Spring and Autumn
and Warring States periods (16th century-221 B.C.) there
were ever closer contacts among these nationalities, leading eventually to national assimilation among them. During this period the Huaxia people came into existence
through a merger of the Xia, Zhou and Shang nationalities with the Qing, Rong, Di, Miao and Man nationalities.

By the time of the Qin Dynasty (221-207 B.C.) China
had become a united, multi-national country. The First
Emperor of Qin, following his unification of the country
in 221 B.C., centralized the multi-national state under a
feudal autocracy.   The Dongyi living along the Huaihe
River, the Nanman in the Changjiang River valley, the
Baiyue living in present-day Guangdong, Guangxi and
Fujian and Zhejiang, Zhurong in the western part of the
country and the various nationalities in Yunnan and Guizhou all came under the rule of the Qin emperor. In order
to maintain his control over these people of various nationalities, he instiued prefectures and counties on the
Central Plains and in other parts of the country.

After the founding of this centralized state power, this unification was strengthened because the development of the productive forces and the interests of the various nationalities demanded it and were opposed to divisions and splits. Although divisions and splits did occur in the history of feudal China, unification was the main trend of historical development. In the long course of the struggle for unification versus division, the country came under successive unified rule during the Han, Sui, Tang, Yuan and Qing dynasties. This led to greater economic contacts and cultural exchanges between the various nationalities, progress in their social systems and speedy development of their economies and culture.

By the Han Dynasty (206 B.C.-A.D. 220), the country had been further unified. This happened when the Huaxia nationality absorbed many other tribes and nationalities of the time to become one nation with an immense population, known as the Han nation. The Huaxia had gradually assimilated those nationalities that were not yet part of the Huaxia during the Qin Dynasty. By the end of the 2nd century B.C. they had unified with the Qiang nationality living in the northwest, and merged with the Wuhuan nationality living in the northeast and the Man nationality on Hainan Island. In 60 B.C., the Han Dynasty set up a "local government of the Western Regions" in modern Xinjiang, a step that led to the unification of more than 30 "city states". Later, the Han also unified with segments of the Southern Xiongnu and Xianbei nationalities living in the north.

After the Han Dynasty, China underwent a period of 300 years of divisions and splits and did not become reunited until the Sui and Tang time (A.D. 581-907). Political, economic and cultural contacts between the national-

ities were strengthened and developed as never before in
the Sui and Tang dynasties. In A.D. 618, following the
demise of the Sui Dynasty, the Tang Dynasty unified the
Eastern Turks living both south and north of the Gobi
Desert and the Western Turks in modern Xinjiang and
Central Asia. The Tang Dynasty established local administrations in which tribal chiefs were granted hereditary offices and empowered to rule in the capacity of
local authorities.

In the Yuan Dynasty (1271-1368), following another
300 years or so of divisions and splits, a new period of
unification began. Genghis Khan and his Mongol suc-
cessors founded an empire and renamed it the Yuan
Dynasty in 1271. They conquered the Southern Song in
1279 to unify the country. Under the Yuan emperors
"provincial governments" were empowered to administer
the areas where minority nationalities lived in the Northeast, Inner Mongolia, Xinjiang, Guangdong, Guangxi,
Yunnan and Guizhou; administrative departments were
put in charge of affairs in Tibet; and offices responsible
for administrative work were established in Penghu and
Taiwan. Moreover, tribal chiefs in Yunnan, Guizhou, Sichuan and Xikang were granted hereditary offices and
empowered to rule in the capacity of local authorities,
thereby forging closer ties between the minority nationalities and the central government.

During the Qing Dynasty (1644-1911) the unification
of various nationalities was further strengthened and
developed. In the north, the Qing unified the various
groups of Mongolians. After putting down rebellions
started by the Mongolian Jungar tribe, reactionary elements among the Uygurs, and the upper classes of Tibet
in collaboration with the Mongolian Jungar tribe in the

areas of Xinjiang and Tibet, the Qing government con-
solidated its control of these areas and protected the unification of the country.   The government also established
a provincial government and county administrations on
the island of Taiwan.   And in the process of fighting aggression by Tsarist Russia, the government strengthened
its administrative work in the northeast, especially among
the minority nationalities living in the drainage area of
the Heilong River.

Thus Chinese history over the past 2,000 years shows
that, in the course of building and development, the
struggle for unification has always stood as a central task
for the whole nation.   Although the principal role in this
great cause of unification had been played by the Han
nationality and important parts have been taken by the
Mongolian and Manchu nationalities, the conditions leading to unification were also implemented by the Xiongnu,
Xianbei, Qidan, Nüzhen, Tibetan, Uygur, Yi, Bai and
other nationalities when they achieved partial unifica-
tions in the places where they resided during the time
when the country was divided.   This is why we say that
the Chinese people have acted in a common effort to build
a united, multi-national country.

(2) ECONOMIC TIES AND CULTURAL EXCHANGES

All the nationalities in China have made sizable contributions to the country's economic and cultural development.   Yet owing to differences in history, geography,
communications and natural conditions, the economy and
culture of the various nationalities developed unevenly.
Generally speaking, the Han people were more advanced,

especially in agriculture, sericulture and metallurgy. But there were many advances of minority nationalities that exerted an influence on the Hans and enriched and further developed the country's economy and culture.

Many minority nationalities based their livelihood on animal husbandry and achieved great skill in raising horses, donkeys and mules. This contributed to the development of a diversified economy in the country. Some minority nationalities in ancient China also reached a fairly high level of agricultural development. These nationalities in what is now Xinjiang were growing, as early as in the Qin and Han dynasties, cereals, mulberry trees, hemp, grape and other crops. Crops such as sorghum, maize, cotton, sesame, grape, watermelon, cucumbers and carrots were all introduced into central China by the nationalities of these western regions.

As far back as in the Tang and Song dynasties (618-1279) there were a number of minority nationalities in Yunnan that had developed water conservancy and irrigation projects on a mass scale at Dali and Dianchi. The Tubos in Tibet also attained a relatively high level of development in growing wheat, barley, buckwheat and kidney bean and in tilling land and crop irrigation.

As early as in the period of Han Dynasty, Guizi, then known as an iron mining centre, supplied metal products to the whole Western Regions. The Xinanyi people particularly showed marvellous workmanship in making hoolowed-out and carved gold and silver articles and jade-inlaid objects. The Xinanyis were experts in mining copper, iron, lead, tin, gold and silver. To the north, the Xiongnu were noted for their skill in making bows, arrowheads, swords and knives. The Zhuang and Dong nationalities reached a high artistic plane with their brocades, and the Li people demonstrated a high skill in cotton spinning and weaving. It was by learning from the Li people that Huang Daopo, a famous weaver of the Yuan Dynasty, improved her technique and popularized it among the people of the Han nationality.

Great contributions were also made by the minority nationalities in China's culture and science. Many beautiful poems, myths, folktales, songs and dances are directly related to them. Among the outstanding literary works by various minority writers are the *Inside History of the Mongols* by a mid-13th century Mongolian writer; the *Biography of King Jagar,* an 11th-century epic of the Tibetans; *Knowledge Gives Happiness,* a long narrative poem of the Uygur people; *Manasi,* the epic of the Kirgiz people; and the long narrative poem by the Sani people of the Yi nationality, *Ashima.* The famous Dunhuang murals, the Yungang and Longmen caves and the Thousand Buddha Caves of Kizir are all creations by artists of the Han, Xianbei, Tubo and other nationalities in the Western Regions. Murals on the cliff of the Huashan Mountain towering over the Zuojiang River in Guangxi are famous works by ancient members of the Zhuang nationality. The lively figures and animals in the murals are of high artistic quality.

The music of the minority nationalities also had its influence in the growth of Chinese music. The well-known "Bayu Dance", dating back to the Han Dynasty, was originally a folk piece of the Ba nationality. The "Ten Books of Music" have been handed down from the Tang Dynasty, most of which can be traced to minority nationalities then living in Guizi and Shule. Among the folk instruments now generally used throughout China are flutes, *pipas,* Hu fiddles, waist drums and copper gongs, all of which came from minority nationalities.

In the field of science and technology, the Ten-Thousand-Year Almanac Calendar published by the Yuan government was compiled by Jamal al-Din, a member of the Hui nationality. His contributions to astronomy included the founding of an observatory in Datu (Beijing) and the design of several scientific instruments, including an armillary sphere. The book *Essentials of Agriculture, Sericulture, Clothing and Food* was written by Uygur agronomist, Lu Mingshan, during the Yuan Dynasty; and *Quick Method for Determining Segment Areas* was by the celebrated Mongol methmatician, Ming Antu, in the Qing Dynasty. All these contributions served the cause of unification and the gradual strengthening of China.

(3) HEROIC STRUGGLE

The minority nationalities have a great revolutionary tradition. They have made significant contributions in the struggle against class oppression and national oppression under various dynasties, and in the struggle against foreign imperialism and colonialism.

During the long course of feudal society, peasant uprisings against feudal rule incessantly broke out. Some of these uprisings were initiated by people of the minority nationalities, and some were started by the Hans in coordination with people of the minority nationalities. Among the best known of these was the great uprising started by people of the Yi, Bai and Han, involving more than 100,000 people in Yunnan; the uprising by people of the Yao in Datengxia during the Ming Dynasty (1368-1644); and the uprising, also during the Ming Dynasty, led by Ma Shouying of the Hui nationality, who joined forces with Li Zicheng and Zhang Xianzhong. In their struggle against national and class oppression, the minority nationalities dealt heavy blows to the feudal ruling class and thus accelerated the development of modern Chinese society.

The various nationalities of China shared a common fate, being subjected to oppression and exploitation by imperialism, feudalism and bureaucrat capitalism. The more than 100-year history of the modern Chinese democratic revolution shows that the various national minority peoples fought beside the Han people to carry out a struggle against the foreign invaders and domestic reactionaries. The Taiping Heavenly Kingdom Revolution, which began in 1851, symbolized the awakening of the Chinese people. It was a great revolutionary movement against imperialism and feudalism started by the people of the Han, Zhuang, Yao, Hui, Miao, Dong and Yi nationalities. During the Revolution of 1911 that overthrew the Qing Dynasty and in the May 4th Movement of 1919 there were also a great number of the people of the Zhuang, Hui, Mongolian and other nationalities fighting alongside the Han people.

In 1921 the Chinese Communist Party was founded. From then on the revolutionary struggles of various nationalities entered a new stage. During the period from the 1920s to the 1930s there were armed clashes against the rule of the Northern warlords and the Kuomintang government by the people of the Mongolian, Hui, Zhuang, Miao, Manchu, Korean, Li and other nationalities. Revolutionary bases were established in the area of Zuojiang and Youjiang rivers inhabited by the Zhuang and Yao nationalities, in the Li area on Hainan Island, and in the Miao and Tujia areas in Hunan and Hubei. In 1935 the Red Army set out on the Long March. Going through areas inhabited by the Miao, Dong, Bouyei, Yi, Tibetan, Qiang and Hui nationalities, the revolutionary army exerted a great influence on them. It helped them organize their own armed forces and establish revolutionary bases. Many working people of the minority nationalities joined the Red Army.

In 1937, after the outbreak of the War of Resistance Against Japan, many persons of minority origin joined the Eighth Route and the New Fourth armies led by the Chinese Communist Party. They fought many heroic battles. In the Northeast the United Anti-Japanese Army was composed of the fine sons and daughters of the Han, Manchu, Korean, Mongolian, Hui, Daur, Ewenki, Oroqen and Hezhen nationalities. On Hainan Island the Qiong-ya Column was formed of Han, Li and Miao people. In the Shaanxi-Gansu-Ningxia Border Region there was a cavalry regiment of Hui people. In Hebei and the Bohai Sea there was a detachment composed of Hui people. In the base area at Daqingshan there was a gurrilla unit formed of Mongolians. And in Yunnan there was the border detachment formed by people of the Han and other nationalities.

During the War of Liberation (1945-49), the revolutionary struggle of the people of all nationalities reached its highest point. Led by the Chinese Communist Party, the people of the various nationalities joined in the decisive battle to overthrow imperialism, feudalism are bureaucrat capitalism. They fought alongside the People's Liberation Army, an army of the people of all nationalities, until the whole mainland was liberated and the country unified.

3. THE MINORITY NATIONALITIES

(1) NORTHEAST CHINA AND INNER MONGOLIA: MANCHU, KOREAN, HEZHEN, MONGOLIAN, DAUR, EWENKI AND OROQEN.

The Manchus. This minority nationality has a population of 4,299,159.* The majority live in Liaoning Province, and the rest are in Jilin, Heilongjiang and Hebei, Inner Mongolia and Xinjiang, as well as in Beijing, Chengdu, Xi'an, Guangzhou and other big and middle-sized cities.

The Manchus have their own oral and written language. The written form, created towards the end of the 16th century, uses the Mongolian lettering system. It belongs to the Manchu-Tungusic group of the Altaic language family. In the 1640s, because of their many contacts with the Han people, most Manchus also learned the language and written script of the Han people.

The ancestry of the Manchus can be traced more than 2,000 years back to the Sushen tribe, and later to the Yilou, Wuji, Mohe and Nüzhen tribes. Living in the Northeast and practising Shamanism, they maintained frequent contacts with people on the Central Plains. In the middle of the 16th century, the Nüzhen chief, Nurhachi, a great political and military strategist, unified the

---

* According to the census of 1982, the same below.

various Nüzhen tribes. He initiated the Eight Banner System of military organization and founded the Later Kin. In 1635, after changing the name of his nationality from "Hüzhen" to "Manchu", he also adopted the dynastic title of "Qing". In 1644, he marched his forces southward and overthrew the Ming Dynasty, unifying the country under the Qing Dynasty.

Since the Manchus originally lived in the forests and mountains, they excelled in archery and horsemanship. At the age of six or seven, children were taught the art of bird shooting with wooden bows; teenagers were taught to ride horseback in full hunting gear, racing through the forests and mountains. Women as well as men were skilled horse riders.

The Manchus were also quite muscial. Wearing leopard skin, they often sang and danced to the accompaniment of flutes and drums. The long novel *A Dream of Red Mansions* is by the great Manchu novelist Cao Xueqin. It is a great work of realism in Chinese classical literature. It has even won its place in the history of world literature. Manchu jade carving and walnut carving are also noted for their fine workmanship.

The traditional dress for Manchu men was a narrow-cuffed short jabket over a long gown with a belt at the waist. Men let the hair on the back of their heads grow long and wore it hanging down in a plait. Women had their hair coiled on top of their heads and wore earrings, long gowns and embroidered shoes. Children were required to pay formal respects to their elders regularly, once in every three to five days.

The Koreans. This nationality has a population of 1,763,870. Most of them live in Jilin, Heilongjiang, Liaoning provinces, while the rest are found in a number of cities. The biggest community of Koreans is in the Yanbian Korean Autonomous Prefecture of Jilin Province. They have their own oral and written language.

The Koreans, most of whom are farmers, moved into China from the Korean Peninsula during the period between the late 17th and middle 19th centuries. They were the first people to set up paddy fields in the Northeast. They are experts in growing rice and produce a white, creamy and nutritious variety.

The Koreans enjoy music and are often seen in the fields and at construction sites dancing to the accompaniment of long drums. On Spring Festival and Mid-Autumn Festival, their communities ring with the music of plucked Gaya and flutes. Among the beautiful dances they perform are *Happy Farming Season, Balancing Water on the Head, Fan Dance* and *Long Drum Dance.*

The traditional Korean costume is white in colour. Women wear short jackets tied with a long ribbon and long straight or wrap-over skirts that hang to their feet. Men wear sleeveless jackets over wide-legged trousers.

Rice and millet are their chief food staples. Glutinous rice dough, cold noodles, pickled vegetables, soup made of soya sauce and hot peppers are favourite items in their diet. Their houses are built of wood with roofs sloping down on four sides. In these they have platforms built of bricks and stone slabs. This is where people sit without their shoes after they enter a house.

The Hezhens. This nationality, numbering 1,476, is the smallest in China. They live in Tongjiang, Fuyuan and Naohe counties along the Heilong River in Heilongjiang Province. They have no written language of their own. Their oral language belongs to the Manchu-Tungusic group of the Altaic language family. For the most part they use the oral and written language of the Han people. They also practise Shamanism, and their principal occupation is fishing.

The Hezhens like to call themselves "Nanai" or "Nabei", a word that means "natives". By ancestry, they are closely related to the Manchus. They are noted for their skill in fishing, especially their ability to spear fish. They are also good hunters of martens and deer, and they ski over ice and snow in their pursuit of the wild beasts.

Before the Qing Dynasty, the Hezhens lived in a communal society. They owned their fishing grounds, mountains and forests communally, and they distributed the fruit of their labour equally. But the fishing grounds eventually became the property of individuals. By the time of Liberation, the Hezhen people, then numbering only about 300 individuals, had become almost extinct because of long oppression and exploitation by warlords, landlords and foreign aggressors. Their numbers have increased since Liberation.

In the past, the Hezhens lived principally on fish. They make a particularly delicious roast fish dish. Now they have added grain to their diet. Instead of wearing hides of fish, deer and roe deer as they did in the past, they now wear woven clothing throughout the four seasons.

The Mongolians. This nationality numbers 3,411,657 and is, for the most part, distributed throughout the Inner Mongolia Autonomous Region, although some members live in Liaoning, Jilin, Heilongjiang, Xinjiang, Qinghai, Gansu, Ningxia, Hebei, Henan, Sichuan, Yunnan and Beijing. They are believers of Lamaism, and have their own oral and written language. They use three dialects: Inner Mongolian, Barag-buriad and Uirad. The language belongs to the Mongolian group of the Altaic language family. The written script was developed in the 13th century from ancient Huigu. It was later revised into the form used today.

The Mongolians, or "Mongol Shiwei" as they were known in early times, were originally herdsmen roaming the banks of the Ergun River. They moved later to the grasslands of western Mongolia. By the 12th century they were living on the upper reaches of the Onon, Kerulen and Tula rivers and in the Hentey Mountains. Early in the 13th century Genghis Khan (1162-1227) organized a powerful Mongolian army. He conquered various Mongolian tribes to found the Mongol Khanate. His successor, Kublai Khan, (1215-1294) succeeded in conquering the Southern Song Dynasty and unifying China under the Yuan Dynasty.

The Mongolians have a fine cultural tradition. The *Inside History of Mongolia* is the earliest work in their history. They have compiled many Mongolian dictionaries, and have produced important works in natural science and medicine. In addition, they have translated many classical literary works from Han and Tibetan into the Mongolian language. Their folk tales and ballads, which are many, were handed down orally for many generations.

The grasslands of Inner Mongolia are often called the "homeland of songs and dances". Among the most characteristic Mongolian dances are the *Horse Sabre* dance, a vigorous number in easy style, *Winecup* and *Chopsticks,* both performed with brisk steps. The Mongolian horsehead guitars produce low, wide and melodious sounds that are quite pleasant.

Because of their nomadic life style, the Mongolians used to live exclusively in yurts. But, since Liberation,

they have begun to live in permanent settlements. Beef,
mutton, dairy products and rice serve as their main food.
The costumes of Mongolian women are multicoloured.
Both men and women wear long and wide gowns with silk
bands at their waists. The men also wear hats or turbans,
and little ornamental knives are attached to their waistbands. The women wear long braids, intertwined with
red and blue fabric. In winter both men and women wear
leather coats, fur caps, and felt boots to protect them from
the cold.

"Nadam" (a Mongolian word meaning "recreation")
is the name for the traditional Mongolian mass gathering,
or fair. It is held every year during the slack season that
lasts from June to September. At the fair, people participate in wrestling, horse racing, archery, singing, dancing
and the exchange of goods.

The Daurs. This nationality numbers 94,017. They
are distributed in the main in Inner Mongolia, Heilongjiang Province and the Xinjiang Uygur Autonomous Region. The biggest community is in the Molidawa Daur
Autonomous Banner, situated on the left bank of the Nen-
jiang River. The Daurs are believers in Shamanism. They
have no written script, and their oral language belongs
to the Mongolian group of the Altaic language family. Most
Daurs use the Han script; a small number know Mongolian.

Historical records show that the Daurs trace their
ancestry back to the ancient Qidan tribe. They gave themselves the name Daur.

They mainly engage in agriculture and animal husbandry, as well as in fishing and hunting.

Their culture and arts, with a varied and long history, are rich and colourful. The women participate in

group singing and dancing on festival days, the girls wearing their hair in shiny braids and flowers of all colours and married women in their bridal clothes and their hair in tall buns adorned with pink flowers. Unique to this nationality are ball matches (balls of oxen hair) that are held between the young men on the same occasions. The Daurs are also noted for their practice of helping each other, and for their respect for the aged.

The Ewenkis. This nationality numbers 13,000 persons distributed in seven banners of the Inner Mongolia Autonomous Region and in Nahe County of Heilongjiang Province. They have no written language, but their oral language is composed of three dialects. These belong to the Manchu-Tungusic group of the Altaic language family. Ewenki herdsmen generally speak Mongolian, while Ewenkis living in agricultural areas and places near the mountains generally use the Han language. Most of them are believers of Shamanism, although some of them believe in Lamaism and others in the Orthodox Eastern Religion.

The name Ewenki is that by which the people call themselves. It means "people living deep in the mountains and forests". They have traced their ancestry to the "Shiwei" tribe living at the time of Northern Wei Dynasty (386-534) on the upper and middle reaches of the Heilong River. During the Tang Dynasty, they developed a close relationship with the "Ju" tribesmen, then herding deer in the forests northeast of Lake Baikal.

The Ewenkis are noted for the ability in livestock breeding. They are experts in knowing the characteristics and habits of different kinds of livestock and different kinds of grass on the pastureland. Because of their experience in hunting and herding deer in the forests, they also have a good knowledge of the habits of wild beasts.

Folk dance performances given by the Ewenkis are quite distinctive in their bold, forceful, and rhythmic style. On festive days, they hold parties in celebration where the "Ahanbai" dance and "Zhehuileng" dance are performed. Their folk songs and music carry a strong flavour of the grassland.

The Oroqens. Numbering 4,132 members, the Oroqens are distributed mainly in the Oroqen Autonomous Banner, Hulun Buir League, of the Inner Mongolian Autonomous Region and in Huma County of Heilongjiang Province. They have no written language, and their oral language belongs to the Tungus branch of the Manchu-Tungusic group of the Altaic language family. They are believers in Shamanism.

The name Oroqen, a name by which they call themselves, means "people living high up in the mountains". Hunting is their principal occupation, apart from fishing and gathering food. A common saying among the Oroqens is that "men defy high mountains while women do not fear work that calls for meticulous care". Children at a tender age are taken hunting in the mountains by their elders, and teenagers go hunting alone. Even the women demonstrate their worth by their good horsemanship and marksmanship in hunting, although they spend most of their time at household chores. The women produce excellent embroidery work and needlework. They make daily articles and utensils of birch bark, as they have done for centuries. These are beautifully designed, fine in line and many in variety. Like many other nationalities the Oroqens are highly musical.

Before Liberation the Oroqens had adopted forms of private ownership, although they also retained traces of their earlier primitive communal society. But it was only after Liberation that they built permanent settlements, thus abandoning their past life style. After settling down, they have become protecters of precious wild life, deer farmers and hunters of other animals.

(2) NORTHWEST CHINA:
HUI, DONGXIANG, TU, SALAR, BONAN, YUGUR, UYGUR, KAZAK, KIRGIZ, XIBE, TAJIK, OZBEK, RUSSIAN AND TATAR.

The Huis.   One of the biggest minority nationalities in China, the Huis have a population of 7,219,352 and are found in most counties and cities of the country.   The largest concentrations are in the Ningxia Hui Autonomous Region, in the provinces of Qinghai, Gansu, Henan, Hebei, Shandong and Yunnan, and in the Xinjiang Uygur Autonomous Region. The Huis are primarily farmers, though some engage in commerce and in the handicraft industry. In economy and culture they have forged close ties with the Han people. They use the oral and written language of the Hans. But in the field of religion they also use words and phrases from the Persian and Arabian languages since Islamism is their common religious faith.

Hui is the shortened form for the Huihui nationality. Its origins were in the 7th century when small numbers of Arabs and Persians came to China for purposes of trade. Gradually more and more of these people settled in China. Then early in the 13th century, large numbers of people from Central Asia, Persia and the Arab world came as immigrants to China. By intermarrying with Hans, Uygurs and Mongolians, they formed a new people known as Huihuis.

History shows that the Hui people have produced many outstanding scientists and great statesmen. These include the great statesman Sayyied Ejell of the Yuan Dynasty, the famous navigator Zheng He and progressive thinker Li Zhi during Ming Dynasty and others, who contributed their part to the cultural and scientific development of the country.

The Huis wear much the same clothing as the Han people, although the men have a preference for white or black caps and the women for turbans that have recently been replaced by a piece of white cloth or a white towel wrapped around the head.

Among their traditional festivals are Mawlid al-Nabi (birthday of Mohammed), the Festival of Fast-Breaking and Corban. On festival days they usually pay each other visits and give gifts of fried dough.

The Dongxiangs. This nationality has a population of 279,397 distributed in Gansu, Xinjiang and Ningxia. More than half of the Dongxiangs live in compact communities in the Dongxiang Autonomous County of Gansu Province. Their language belongs to the Mongolian group of the Altaic language family. Most Dongxiangs are bilingual, with a good command of the Han language. They use the written script of the Han people. Islamism is their religion. They engage in agriculture and animal husbandry.

Legends tell us that the Dongxiangs had their origin among the Mongols who moved in the 13th century into the area of modern Linxia and Dongxiang in Gansu Province. They became a separate nationality by intermarrying over a long period with the Huis and Hans living nearby.

The Dongxiang now have much the same customs, habits, and religious faith as the Hui people do, although they have retained some customs of the Mongolians. The women, for example, wear gowns, as Mongolian women do; the men generally like to wear black flat-topped caps, as the Huis do.

"Huaer" is the name of the musical form used by the Dongxiang people. Many of these people are good singers and composers of this form of music. Among the Dongxiangs there are also many ancient stories and narrative poems that have been handed down from generation to generation.

The Tus. This nationality has a population of 159,426, mainly distributed in the Huzhu Tu Autonomous County of Qinghai Province, in the Minhe, Datong, Ledu and Menyuan areas of Qinghai Province, and in the Tianzhu area of Gansu Province. Their spoken language belongs to the Mongolian group of the Altaic language family, and they commonly use the written script of the Han people.

The Tus call themselves "Mongol" or "Qagan Mongol" (white Mongol), which indicates their blood lineage with the Mongolians. It is said that their ancestors were a unit of Mongol troops under the command of General Gerelt at the time of Genghis Khan. They were stationed in today's Huzhu County and intermarried with the Hor residents there to become a separate nationality. Some evidence of this has been found in historical records.

At first the Tus engaged in animal husbandry, but by the Ming Dynasty they had changed to agriculture. Tu men and women wear embroidered jackets with tall collars. The men also wear cloth robes and embroidered felt hats, while the women wear black vests over their gowns and tube-shaped, flat-topped felt hats. The women braid their hair and wear coral and pearl ornaments.

The Tus are good dancers and singers and they have a fine tradition in literature and art, their folk literature having been passed orally from generation to generation. They are highly skilled in artistic ornamentation, and the doors and windows of their houses and temples are beautifully engraved with pictures of oxen, sheep and cereal.

The Salars. This nationality has a population of 69,102, among whom 90 per cent live in the Xunhua Salar Autonomous County in eastern Qinghai Province. The rest are distributed in Hualong County, Qinghai Province, and in Linxia, Gansu Province. Their language belongs to the Turkic group of the Altaic language family, and they have no written script of their own. They generally use the Han script. Their religious faith is Islamism. They engage in agriculture, and have a well-developed gardening art.

Historically, the Salars were a group of people who moved from Samarkand in Central Asia during the Yuan Dynasty into today's Xunhua County, Qinghai Province. During the long period of history they intermixed with the Hans, Tibetans and Huis living in the surrounding area, and thus gradually came to form a new people.

Their folk tales are rich and colourful. Their ballads have been handed down orally over the centuries. They have a particularly beautiful folk song, "Huaer", that they sing in the Han language.

The Salars and the Huis have much the same customs. The women wear turbans and colourful garments with black vests over them. The men wear black or white flat-topped, round caps, and sheep skin jackets. Particularly good at needlework, the women often embroider pillows, shoes and socks with floral designs.

The Bonans. With a population of 9,027, living in compact community in the Linxia area of Gansu Province, the Bonans have a language that belongs to the Mongolian group of the Altaic language family. However, most Bonans speak and use the language and written script of the Han people. Their religion is Islamism.

The Bonans began during the Yuan Dynasty as a unit of Mongol troops stationed on garrison duty in Gansu Province. They engaged in land reclamation and herding, and as they intermarried with the Huis, Hans, Tibetans and Tus living in the surrounding areas, they developed into a new people.

Today they mainly engage in agriculture, with some handicraft industries as sideline occupations. The waist knives that they make are well-known products of these handicraft industries.

The Bonans are quite musically inclined. Their musical instruments include wind and string instruments. They have many folk songs and feasting tunes, and their dances are rhythmic, bold and unconstrained, much like Tibetan dances.

The Yugurs. This group has a population of 10,569 distributed mainly in the Sunan Yugur Autonomous County and Huangnibao of Jiuquan County, Gansu Province. Owing to historical conditions, they have three languages: Yugur (Yaohuer) belonging to the Turkic group of the Altaic language family; Yugur (Engeer) belonging to the Mongolian group of the Altaic language family; and Han. The last serves as the general medium for communication. Lamaism is their religious faith.

The Yugurs originated from an ethnic group known in the Tang Dynasty as Huigu. They tended stock along the Ergun River. By the mid-9th century they had

moved westward and settled in an area along the Gansu
Corridor, west of the Huanghe River. During the long
period from the 11th to the 16th centuries, some of the
Huigus intermarried with people of other nationalities in
the surrounding areas and thus gradually became the new
nationality known as the Yugurs, who live today in the
area from Dunhuang to Hami.

The Yugurs engage mainly in livestock breeding, although they also do some farming. Before Liberation
their society contained traces of a feudal tribal system in
the form of primitive tribal organizations. Their society
also contained exploitation and class oppression under
feudal rule.

In the past, the Yugurs lived in tents woven of goat's
wool. But today most of them live in mud houses, group-
ed in settlements. Their folktales, legends, stories, ballads
and proverbs are rich and colourful. Their plain and
beautiful folk songs are sung in a unique way.   They also
show outstanding talent in the plastic arts.   Woollen bags
and carpets made by them are covered with beautiful
designs.

The Uygurs. This nationality has a population of
5,957,112 distributed in the Xinjiang Uygur Autonomous
Region and in Taoyuan and Changde counties of Hunan
Province. About 80 per cent live in closely knit communities in Hotan, Kashi, Aksu and Korla in Xinjiang.
Their language belongs to the Turkic group of the Altaic
language family.   They have two systems of writing, one
in Arabic phonetic letters and another in a recently developed romanized script.   Islamism is their religion.

The name of the Uygur means "unity" or "alliance".
Their ancestry can be traced to that of an ethnic group by
the name "Dingling" that lived in the 3rd century B.C.

by grazing herds in the area south of Lake Baikal. Later they took the name of "Tiele" by which they were known during the Tang Dynasty. They went into alliance with other tribes to fight against the Turks in the 7th century. This was known as the alliance of "Huihe". They later took the name of "Huigu". By the mid-9th century, most the Huigus had moved to the area where they live today. They intermixed over a long period with other peoples such as the Tubos, Qidans and Mongolians, gradually becoming the nationality known as Uygurs today.

It took the Uygurs a long time to switch from stock breeding to agriculture. They now specialize in growing cotton and wheat, and they are skilled at growing melons and fruit. Grapes from Tupan and watermelons from Hami have won fame throughout the world.

The Uygurs have produced a fine heritage in culture and art with unique characteristics of their own. The long narrative poem *Knowledge Gives Happiness* and *A Turkic Dictionary*, handed down from the 11th century, are important works used today for studying the ancient history, culture and language of the Uygur people. They have a great variety of folktales, fables, proverbs, dances and songs. *Twelve Mukamu*, composed of 340 verses, is one of their most popular epic songs. Beautiful, light and brisk in step, their dances are fast and involve many changes in movement. The traditional dances "Balancing Bowls", "Big Drum Dance", "Iron Ring Dance" and "Puta Dance" are the most often performed. "Sainaimu" is another folk dance that is generally enjoyed.

Flour, corn and rice are the staples of the Uygur diet. Tea with milk is their favourite drink. Baked cakes made of flour and corn are generally served at meals. Pillau, a special dish of this nationality, is made of mutton, sheep

fat, carrots, raisins, onions and rice. It is eaten with the
fingers. On festive days, guests and friends are honoured
with pillau.

The men traditionally wear long stripped robes without buttons and tied with a waistband. The women wear
long braids, long skirts and wide-sleeved, bright-coloured
garments covered by an outer black vest. Both men and
women, wear small multi-coloured four-cornered caps.

The Kazaks. This group has a population of 907,582
distributed mainly in the Ili Kazak Autonomous Prefecture, the Mori· Kazak Autonomous County and the Barkol
Kazak Autonomous County north of the Tianshan Mountains in the Xinjiang Uygur Autonomous Region. A
smaller number live in the Aksay Kazak Autonomous
County in Gansu Province and the Haixi Mongolian, Tibetan and Kazak Autonomous Prefecture in Qinghai Province. Their language belongs to the Turkic group of the
Altaic language family. They have a written script devised in 1959 on the basis of the Latin alphabet, which was
substituted for the former one based on the Arabic alphabet.

During the 1st century B.C. the Kazaks lived in the Ili
River valley and in the area near Lake Issyk. They were
then known as Wusuns. In the 6th century a branch of
Turks moved into the area and established a Turkic
Khanate there. By the 12th century there were also Qi-
dans living there, and in the 13th century, Mongolians.
In the long course of contacts with these people the Wu-
suns gradually grew into the nationality known as the
Kazaks.

The Kazak people mainly engage in animal husbandry. The Yili River valley where the Kazak live in
compact communities is known for its fine Ili horse and

Kunas stud sheep.   They live in yurts in spring, summer and autumn, but live in mud houses in the winter. Baked flour and corn cakes, fried dough, noodles, boiled mutton, sausage made of horse meat, tea with milk, horse milk and cream are among their favourite foods.

In accordance with their nomadic life, they generally use hides for their clothing.   The men wear great coats made of sheepskin or fur trousers tied with a waistbank. They sport little knives held in place by their belts.   The women wear beautiful silk vests, dresses, and long, baggy trousers tied at the bottom.   Their caps are made of three pieces of fox skin.   Both men and women wear leather boots.   The caps for young girls are decorated with the feather of an owl.

The Kazaks are by nature warm-hearted and straight-forward.   Friends and visitors are received with great hospitality.   Sheep are slaughtered in their honour, and guests are generally awarded with sheep heads at a meal.

The Kazaks have produced a fine cultural heritage with distinct characteristics of its own.   There are many folk singers, who not only sing but also collect folk songs. The Dombira, a plucked string instrument developed by this nationality, produces beautiful accompaniments for the folk singers as they express different moods of feeling.   Traditional recreational activities, such as horse racing, wrestling, "Girl Chase" and sheep chase, are held in autumn every year.

The Kirgizs. This nationality has a population of 113,999, of which about 80 per cent live in close communities in the Kizilsu Kirgiz Autonomous Prefecture in the southwestern Xinjiang Uygur Autonomous Region. Others live in Tekes, Zhaosu and Emin counties in northern Xinjiang; in Fuyu County of Heilongjiang Province;

and in Hotan, Pishan, Shache, Taxkorgan and Kashi in Xinjiang. Their language belongs to the Turkic group of the Altaic language family. Its former written script was worked out on the basis of Arabic alphabet, but a new written script, based on the Latin alphabet, was devised after Liberation. Han and Uygur are also commonly used by them for communication. Most of the Kirgizs worship Islamism, but a small number worship Lamaism.

The forefathers of the Kirgizs were an ethnic group living on the upper reaches of the Yenisei River, known by the name of "Likun" or "Jiankun" during the Western Han Dynasty. In the mid-6th century there was another ethnic group, also forefathers of the Kirgizs, by the name of "Xiajiasi". This group was under the rule of the Turkic Khanate. In the long course of frequent contacts with the Qidans, Mongolians and Huigus, during the period from the Yuan to the Ming Dynasty, the two groups grew into the nationality as it is known today.

The Kirgizs mostly engage in animal husbandry, with some agriculture.

Following long traditions, the Kirgiz men wear round-collared shirts and tall felt hats. The women wrap their heads in scarfs and wear dresses, baggy trousers, and black vests. Young girls wear embroidered caps sporting a tassel.

The Kirgizs are a gifted people with a wealth of poems, songs, legends, proverbs and fables. Crystallizations of their wisdom are widely circulated. Among these is the epic story, *Manas*. They take great interest in painting and woodcuts. Popular among them is the three-stringed plucked Qomuz, which they use to accompany their many folk songs. They also often hold traditional sports events.   These include sheep chase, wrestling and horse racing.

The Xibes. This nationality has a population of 83,629 distributed mainly in the Qapqal Xibe Autonomous County in the Ili Kazak Autonomous Prefecture of Xinjiang.   The Xibes are also found in the two counties of Huocheng and Gongliu near the Ili River in Xinjiang, in Shenyang, Yixian and Fengcheng in Liaoning Province, and in Huyu County in Jilin Province.   Their language belongs to the Manchu branch of the Manchu-Tungusic group of the Altaic language family. It is said that they formerly had their own written script although this has long fallen into disuse.   Today the Xibes living in northeast China use Manchu and Han, while those living in Xinjiang generally use Uygur and Kazak. They are believers in Shamanism.

At one time the Xibes lived in northwest Jilin Province, east of the Greater Hinggan Mountains.   But in the 17th century they were incorporated by the Qing government into the Eight Banners System of the three provinces of northeast China.   In 1964, the 29th reigning year of Qianlong, the Qing government had some 1,000 officers and men of Xibe origin transferred with their dependents to the south bank of the Ili River to strengthen the garrison forces in Xinjiang.   Organized into eight "niulu" (units), known as "Xibe battalions", they opened up wasteland and grew food grain, making this place their homeland.

The Xibes living in Xinjiang are good horse riders and archers.   They wear clothing similar to that of the Manchus.   The men wear long gowns and short jackets made of blue, black or brown cloth, and round caps.   The women wear long slit skirts, white socks and embroidered shoes.   Young girls wear long braids, but married women have their braids twined around their heads.

Owing to historical differences, the Xibes in northeast China live more or less as the Hans and Manchus do in terms of food, clothing and housing.   Those living in Xinjiang maintain their own custom and habits.

The Tajiks.   This group has a population of 26,503 of whom 60 per cent are concentrated on the eastern plateau of Pamirs in the Taxkorgan Tajik Autonomous County of the Xinjiang Uygur Autonomous Region.   The remainder live in Shache, Zepu, Yecheng and Pishan in Xinjiang.   Their language belongs to the Iranian group of the Indo-European language family.   They have no written script, and sometimes make use of the written language of the Uygurs.   They are Islams in religious faith.

The word "Tajik" means "crown".   It had been applied to this nationality by the 11th century.   The nationality resulted from a merger of people living in Xinjiang since early times with groups of people who moved there from west of the Pamir.

The Tajiks who live in mountainous areas engage mainly in animal husbandry, while those living on the plains engage in agriculture.

The men among the Tajiks wear collarless long jackets, leather boots and small round caps or turbans; the women wear dresses, coloured trousers and round embroidered caps sewn with flaps at the back to protect their necks from the cold.   On festive days and happy occasions the women wear long braids, necklaces adorned with silver and shell ornaments, embroidered caps with silver chains, big earrings, necklaces and beautiful boots and belts.

Tajik folk literature in the form of poems, songs, legends, stories and proverbs are found in great abundance. The eagle appears in their folk literature as a symbol of heroism, and Nay (flutes) made of eagle bones are their favourite musical instrument. Many of their dances also imitate the movements of eagles.

The Ozbeks. This nationality has a population of 12,453 distributed in many counties and cities of the Xinjiang Uygur Autonomous Region, but mostly concentrated in Yining, Tacheng, Kashi, Urumqi, Shache and Yecheng. Their language belongs to the Turkic group of the Altaic language family, and they once used a written script based on Arabic Alphabet. Now, in substitution for this, they use the written scripts of the Uygurs and the Kazaks. They worship in the Islam faith.

The Ozbek nationality originated as the Ozbek of the Jinzhang Khanate during the 14th century. Later, they used Ozbek as the name of the khanate. By the 15th century, there were groups of Ozbeks scattered throughout various parts of Central Asia. They allied themselves under the name of the Ozbek Coalition. In the 17th century large numbers of them from Central Asia began to settle in Xinjiang. Most were engaged in trade. They formed themselves into trade caravans that travelled on the Silk Road between Central Asia and Xinjiang. A small number also engaged in handicraft industries, agriculture and animal husbandry.

The Ozbeks live more or less as the Uygurs do in terms of customs, clothing, food, housing and recreational activities. They are good musicians, and they use a variety of musical instruments. One of these, the triangular Sernay, is a stringed instrument unique to this nationality. The Ozbeks also take great interest in "poem contests" held every year when apple trees are in full blossom.

The Russians. There are 2,935 Russians distributed in Ili, Tacheng, Altay and Urumqi in the Xinjiang Uygur Autonomous Region. Some also live in the Inner Mongolia Autonomous Region. Their language belongs to the Slavic group of the Indo-European language family, and they believe in the Orthodox Eastern Church.

The Russians first moved into China from Tsarist Russia in the 18th century. By the 19th century and just before and after the outbreak of the October Revolution Russians came in increasing numbers. They live much as Russians do in the Soviet Union. Most of them work in the transport and handicraft industries. Some are also engaged in agriculture, and others work at gardening, animal husbandry and apiculture. Those living in the countryside have reclaimed much of the wasteland along the banks of the Ili and Tekes rivers.

The Tatars. This group has a population of 4,127, living in Yining, Tacheng and Urumqi in the Xinjiang Uygur Autonomous Region. Their language belongs to the Turkic group of the Altaic language family. In the past they had a written script based on Arabic alphabet, but now they use the Uygur and Kazak written scripts. Islamism is their religious faith.

The Tatars, also known as "Dadans", were formerly a tribal people under the domain of the Turkic Khanate during the Tang Dynasty. By the 13th century they were vanquished by the Mongols. It is recorded that they grew into a nationality from a merger of the Buglas, Kypchaks and Mongols. During the 15th century they were principally residents of the Kashan Khanate. From the mid-19th century onwards, some of the Tatars from Central Asia began to move into China and settle in Xinjiang. Most of them are engaged in trade, animal husbandry and educational work.

Because the Tatars have a long relationship of living in the same area as the Uygurs and Kazaks, they share many aspects of common culture. Zhuafan (rice eaten with the fingers); cakes made of cheese, rice and dried apricots; and cakes made of pumpkins, meat and rice that are soft and crisp inside out are foods peculiar to this nationality. "Knaisima", made of fermented honey, is their favourite drink.

The Tatars are noted for their grassland music, rhythmic, bold and unconstrained. On festive days and happy occasions they hold mass dance contests.

(3) SOUTHWEST CHINA:
   TIBETAN, MOINBA, LHOBA, QIANG, YI, BAI, HANI, DAI, LISU, VA, LAHU, NAXI, JINGPO, BLANG, ACHANG, PUMI, NU, BENGLONG, DRUNG, JINO, MIAO, BOUYEI, DONG, SHUI, AND GELO.

The Tibetans. This nationality has a population of 3,870,068 living in the Tibet Autonomous Region as well as in Sichuan, Qinghai, Gansu and Yunnan provinces. Their language belongs to the Tibeto-Burman group of the Han-Tibetan language family. It is composed of three dialects that represent three different administrative areas, Tibet, Xikang and Anduo. They have a written script that was created in the 7th century and has been used ever since. They worship Lamaism. Before 1959, Tibet maintained a system of feudal serfdom in which the administrative government and religious bodies were integrated. Democratic reforms were introduced in Tibet in 1959, and since then the nationality has gradually embarked on the road of socialism.

The Tibetans refer to themselves as "Poi" and the localities where they reside by names such as "Poiba", "Kamba", "Andowa" and "Gyarongwa". Originally the Tibetans lived in close communities in the area along the Yarlung Zangbo River. During the Tang Dynasty, early in the 7th century, Songzan Gambo of the Yalong tribe ruled over Tubo from his court in Lhasa. In 641 he married Princess Wencheng of the Tang Dynasty. In 701, his successor, Chide Zugdan, married Princess Jincheng of the Tang Dynasty. These royal weddings cemented contacts with the Han people that have continued throughout history in the fields of politics, economics and culture.

Over the long course of historical development, the Tibetan people have produced a great heritage of art and culture. The vast collection of their ancient literature includes a large number of works dealing with history, geography, astronomy, philosophy and medicine, as well as many novels, dramas, poems, folk tales, fables and legends. Their achievement in painting and sculpture reached a high artistic plane, and their architecture is composed of unique edifices built layer upon layer and looking neat, grand and majestic. The majestic 13-storeyed Potala Palace, constructed in the 7th century, towers as high as 170 metres on the Potala Hill. The Tibetans are also highly musical. Their folk songs are many and varied, and deal with a wide range of subjects. They accompany these with their own unique musical instruments.

Parched *qingko* barley or pea flour mixed with tea and butter, a concoction known as *zanba*, is used by the

Tibetan people as their main food. Tea brewed with milk and *qingko* wine is their favourite drinks. In the agricultural areas of Tibet, the men wear wide-collared long gowns with sleeves about half a span longer than their arms. The women wear sleeveless and collarless long gowns, and patterned skirts. Their woollen cloth, named *pulu*, is the material used for this clothing. In the nomadic areas both men and women wear long sheep-skin gowns. In the agricultural areas the people generally live in two-storeyed square houses made of rock, with many windows. They shelter their cattle and store things on the ground floor and live on the top floor. In the nomadic areas the people, both men and women, wear sheep skin all the year round and live in black tents made of yak hair.

During the Fruit-Awaiting Festival in August every year the Tibetans hold grand celebrations for their harvests. At this time national songs and dances are performed widely.

The Moinbas. This group has a population of 6,248 mostly distributed in the area of Moinyu in the southern part of the Tibet Autonomous Region. A small number also live in Medog, Nyingchi and Cona counties in south-eastern Tibet. Their spoken language belongs to the Moinba branch of the Tibeto-Burman group of the Han-Tibetan language family. It includes a number of dialects. More than half of the Moinbas also speak Tibetan and use the Tibetan script for written communication. Their religious faith is Lamaism.

The name "Moinba", formerly used as an epithet by the Tibetans, means "people living in Moinyu". Over a long period of time the Moinbas have intermarried with the Tibetans and forged close ties with them in terms of economy, culture, religious faith, customs and way of life.

The Moinbas mainly engage in agriculture, although some of them work in the areas of forestry, animal husbandry, hunting, and handicraft industries. Before Liberation they were socially and economically in the stage of feudal serfdom, and some even lived in tribal groupings that maintained traces of an earlier primitive communal system.

All the men and women living in the area of Moinyu wear red *pulu* gowns and brown-topped and yellow-rimmed caps or black felt caps made of yak hair. The women also wear white aprons, bracelets, necklaces, and earrings, as well as the skins of calves attached to their backs. But the men and women in the subtropical area of Medog wear long gowns or short jackets. Buckwheat, millet, corn, rice, turnips, *zanba*, *qingko* wine, buttered tea, cheese and hot peppers are all part of their diet. Among their favourite foods are buckwheat cakes baked on thin stone slabs. Their houses are built of wood or bamboo. They are A-shaped and two- to three-storeyed. The ground floor is used for livestock that are fenced in with walls of stone, wood or bamboo. The people live on the top floor.

The Lhobas. These people have a population of 2,065. They mainly live in the area of Loyu in southeastern Tibet, although a small number also live in Mainling, Medog, Zayü, Lhunze and Nagxian counties in Tibet. Their language belongs to the Tibeto-Burman group of the Han-Tibetan language family.

There are great differences between the dialects in various localities. Owing to the lack of a written script, the Lhobas have long kept their records by tying knots and marking notches in wood. Since Liberation some have begun to use the Tibetan script. They generally believe in witchcraft.

The name "Lhobas" comes from an epithet given them by the Tibetans. It means "southerners". The Lhobas call themselves "Bogar", "Ningbo" or "Bangbo". They engage in agriculture as well as hunting. They are exceptionally good at archery. Before Liberation they were extremely poor and many toiled as household slaves. At that time they carried on slash-and-burn cultivation. But after Liberation, because of the social reforms that were introduced, they have made speedy economic progress.

Among the Lhobas corn flour and millet provide the basic diet. Those Lhobas who live near the Tibetans also eat *zanba* and potatoes, and drink buttered tea. Both the Lhoba men and women like to smoke and drink wine. When a good harvest is in sight or when wild game is captured, they hold parties at which they sing and drink toasts to wish each other new successes in life.

The Lhobas dress simply. The men wear long woollen vests and wild ox skins, rattan or bamboo helmets, and bear skin hats. They hang arrows, bows and sabres at their waists. The women wear narrow-sleeved short jackets and woollen skirts, as well as earrings, bracelets, necklaces, knives and plated copper ornaments. The number of ornaments that a woman wears show the amount of wealth accumulated by her family.

The Qiangs. This nationality has a population of 102,768 living mostly in close communities in the Maowen Qiang Autonomous County of the Aba Tibetan Autonomous Prefecture in Sichuan Province, though some live in Wenchuan, Lixian, Heishui and Songpan counties in Sichuan. Their language belongs to the Tibeto-Burman

group of the Han-Tibetan language family, and is divided
into two dialects, southern and northern. They have no
written script, but use that of the Han people. In the past
they believed that all things on earth have a soul and that
white stones placed on roof tops show their respect for
god.

The Qiangs call themselves "Ermas", a term that
means local people. The same term was used by the ancient Hans to mean the nomadic people then roaming in
the western part of the country. During the Qin and Han
dynasties there was a group of tribal people named Ran-
mangs, who lived in present-day northwest Sichuan and
who were apparently the ancestors of the Qiangs. From
the time of the Sui and Tang dynasties onwards they had
frequent contacts with the Hans and Tibetans in the
surrounding areas. These contacts and subsequent assim-
ilations eventually gave birth to the present Qiang nationality.

Agriculture is the principal occupation of the Qiangs.
They are good at well digging and show marvellous architectural skill in laying rocks and stones. Before Liberation their economic system was that of feudalism.   In
some places they also practised primitive slash-and-burn
cultivation.

The costumes of the Qiang people are beautifully
made, plain and unique in style. Both men and women
wear long linen shirts and vests made of sheep skins, as
well as turbans and puttees. They live in stockaded villages. Their buildings are square, three-storeyed structures with flat tops, and are traditionally built with rocks
of irregular shapes. They house their livestock on the
ground floor, live on the second floor, and store their grain
on the third floor.

The Yis. This nationality has a population of 5,453,448 distributed in Yunnan, Sichuan and Guizhou, and in the Guangxi Zhuang Autonomous Region. Their language belongs to the Yi branch of the Tibeto-Burman group of the Han-Tibetan language family. It has six different dialects. Before Liberation the Yi people used a pictographic written script of an ancient type. Now they have a new written script, devised and standardized since Liberation.

The Yi people are respectively known as "Nuosu", "Nasu" or "Niesu" depending on the locality where they reside. During the period of Qin and Han dynasties, the Yis lived in the area of Lake Dianchi in Yunnan Province and in the area of Qiongdu of Sichuan Province. By the 8th century they had established the slave state of Nanzhao. In the 13th century and up to Liberation they were known as "Luoluo". Only after Liberation did they adopt the present name of Yi.

Today they engage in agriculture and, in some areas, animal husbandry. They maintained a feudal economy before Liberation everywhere but in Sichuan Province and Nanlang in Yunnan Province, where they still kept a slave system.

The costumes of the Yi people show great variety and differ from place to place. Many of the men and women wear long green or blue gowns, waistbands and blue turbans. The women also wear gowns on which the opennings and edges are embroidered with designs, and their trousers are mounted with floral borders. Those Yis who live in mountainous areas that are often cold have collarless and sleeveless short gowns that are made of sheepskin and woollen cloaks.

The achievements of the Yi people in literature and art include *Ashima*, a long and colourful narrative poem that has been handed down for generations. It describes a young village girl, Ashima, and her fight for freedom and happiness against despotic feudal rulers. *Axi Jumps over the Moon* is the name of a dance popular among these people.

Their Torch Festival held annually from the sixth to the 24th day of the sixth lunar month is a celebration of bumper harvests. The festival begins after nightfall when the villagers turn out en mass with flaming torches in their hands. They set up these pine torches around their fields to frighten away the pests. Then they sing, dance and drink toasts to each other throughout the night, accompanying their songs with *yueqin* (a four-stringed plucked instrument with a full-moon-shaped sound box) and mouth organs.

The Bais. This group has a population of 1,131,124. More than 80 per cent live in communities in the Dali Bai Autonomous Prefecture in Yunnan Province. The remainder live in Bijie County in Guizhou Province and Xichang County in Sichuan Province. Their language belongs to the Yi branch of the Tibeto-Burman group of the Han-Tibetan language family, and they use the written script of the Han people. The Bais generally believe in Buddhism, though some are Protestants and Catholics.

The Bai people call themselves by the name of "Baizi" or "Baini", which means "white people". During the 7th century, there were six tribes known as the Six Zhaos in Yunnan Province. These tribes, by the 8th century, had established a monarchy in Yunnan Province. Some of the Six Zhaos came to have a common language and similar habits and customs. This group developed into the Bai nationality.   Today they engage mainly in agriculture.

The Bai people have made many contributions to science and culture.   By the Tang Dynasty, in the area of Dali, they had already built big water conservancy projects.   They were also skilled in astronomy, calender design and meteorology.   Their literature, history and art works include the *History of the Bai People* written during the Song Dynasty, the *Picture Scroll of Nanzhao* painted by Zhang Shun and Wang Fengzong in 899, and the *Picture Scroll of Dali* painted by Zhang Shengwen in 1172.   Third Month Street, the grand festival of the Bai people, is held from 15th to 20th day of the third lunar month on the foothills of Diancang Mountain, west of Dali City.   During this celebration, the Bais engage in horse racing, archery, singing and dancing, and the exchange of goods.

The Hanis.   This nationality has a population of 1,058,836 living in Yunnan Province mainly in the Honghe Hani and Yi Autonomous Prefecture, the Jiangcheng Hani and Yi Autonomous County, and the Xishuangbanna Dai Autonomous Prefecture, although some Hanis also live in Mujiang, Yuanjiang and Lancang counties.   Composing three dialects, the Hani language belongs to the Yi branch of the Tibeto-Burman group of the Han-Tibetan language family.   They had no written script until 1957, when one based on the Latin alphabet was devised.   In the past they generally believed in polytheism and practised ancestor worship.

The Hani people have called themselves by several different names, including those of "Hani', "Yani", "Kaduo" and "Biyue".   They are people with a long history.   During the 8th century they were derogatorily referred to as "Hemans", or barbarians. But, after Liberation, they decided to call themselves by the name of "Hani".

Agriculture is their principal occupation. They have built layer upon layer of terraced fields on the banks of the Yuanjiang River. Some of these rise 100 layers high, and some even reach the mountain top. They are not only experienced in tilling and building terraced fields according to different kinds of terrain and soil, they are also highly skilled in piping water to the fields to irrigate them.

Their economy before Liberation was unevenly developed. In some places they had a landlord economy and in others a serf economy.

Among the festivals they celebrate are the Tenth Month Festival and the Sixth Month Festival, related to the gathering in of crops. They serve beef with newly harvested boiled rice, and all the villagers dress in their holiday best; young people play on swings; and men enjoy themselves at wrestling.

The Dais. This group has a population of 839,797 living in close communities in the Xishuangbanna Dai Autonomous Prefecture, Dehong Dai and Jingpo Autonomous Prefecture, and the Gengma and Menglian autonomous counties in Yunnan Province. There are also few Dais living in Jinggu, Jingdong, Yuanjiang and Jinping counties of Yunnan. Their language belongs to the Zhuang-Dai branch of the Zhuang-Dong group of the Han-Tibetan language family. It is composed of three dialects, Dehong, Xishuangbanna and Jinping. At one time they had five different kinds of written scripts, but in 1954 these were reformed into a single script. In religion they are Hinayana Buddhists.

The Dai people have been known by many ancient

names, including "Shan", "Jinchi" or "Baiyi", but they call themselves "Daile", "Daina" or "Daiya". They mainly engage in agriculture, and are highly skilled in cultivating rice. Before Liberation most of the Dai areas were in the stage of a serf economy, although some places had reached to the stage of a landlord economy.

The Dai people live in two-storied bamboo stilt houses with balconies, bedrooms and kitchens on the upper floor. The ground floor is used to house poultry and domestic animals and to store grain. Their traditional costumes are bright coloured. The men wear collarless short jackets and long trousers. They also wear turbans on their heads. The women wear short jackets and colourful long skirts, with their hair tied into buns.

The Dais have their own calendar, which begins from A.D. 638. Their Water Sprinkling Festival is traditionally celebrated in the sixth or seventh month of the Dai calendar. On such festive days, people fire rockets, join in dragon-boat racing, and sprinkle water on each other to exchange good wishes. The *Peacock Dance* and *Fish Dance* are among their most popular dances. Their unique musical instruments include elephant-foot drums and gongs.

The Lisus. These people comprise a population of 480,960, who live primarily in close communities in the Nujiang Lisu Autonomous Prefecture in northwest Yunnan Province. Some members of this nationality also live in Lijiang, Baoshan, Diqing, Dali, Dehong and Chuxiong counties in Yunnan, as well as in Xichang and Yanbian counties in Sichuan Province. Their language belongs the Yi branch of the Tibeto-Burman group of the Han-Tibetan language family. They formerly had a rudimentary written script, somewhat imperfect in structure. But in 1957 they devised a new written script based on the Latin alphabet. Most of the Lisu people believe in polytheism. Some are Catholics or Protestants.

In the 7th century, the forefathers of the Lisus were living along the banks of the present-day Jinsha River and in southwestern Sichuan Province. But 400 years ago a number of them moved from there to settle along the Lancang and Nujiang rivers. They engage in agriculture, as well as gathering and hunting. Until Liberation, most of them lived under a feudal economy. But in the area of Nujiang and Dehong they still maintained vestages of a primitive communal system.

The Lisu people traditionally wear black costumes. The women wear short jackets and long skirts, and like to decorate their heads with red-coloured beads and strings of shell ornaments. They also wear multi-coloured necklaces. In the past, when men went on a long journey, they always took bows and arrows with them, the arrows held in bags made of bear hides that were tied to their waists.

The Harvest Festival of the Lisu people falls in October, just half month after their corn crop is harvested. The people celebrate it in every Lisu village with slaughtered pigs, toasts and present exchanges. Bonfire blaze in the villages all night, and the people enjoy themselves with singing and dancing.

The Vas. This nationality has a population of 298,591 living mainly in the Changyuan and Ximeng areas of southwest Yunnan Province. A few also live in the Xishuangbanna Dai Autonomous Prefecture and the Dehong Dai and Jingpo Autonomous Prefecture of Yunnan. Their language belongs to the Cambodian group of Southeast Asian languages, and is composed of three dialects.   They had no written script until 1957 when one was devised on the basis of the Latin alphabet.   Before Liberation the Vas believed in animism.   But there were also Buddhists or Christians among them.

The Vas are among the most ancient recorded people of western Yunnan.   By the 2nd century, the ancestors of the Vas, a people called the Wangs, were already living over a wide area to the north of the Awa Mountains.

Today the Vas principally engage in agriculture and hunting.   Those living in Cangyuan, Gengma and Zhenkang had entered the stage of feudalism before Liberation, while those living in Ximeng, Lancang and Menglian still maintained traces of a primitive communal system.

The men today wear sabres and black turbans.   The women wear short skirts and silver earrings, necklaces and bracelets.   During their Spring Festival, the people visit each other, carrying presents with them, such as bananas and cakes made of glutinous rice.   They hold parties that last for several consecutive days and enjoy themselves in singing and dancing.

The Lahus.   This group has a population of 304,174. Most of them live in close communities in the Lancang Lahu Autonomous County and the Menglian Dai, Lahu and Va Autonomous County of Yunnan Province.   The remainder live in Shuangjiang, Gengma, Simao and Puer counties, Yunnan.   Their language belongs to the Yi branch of the Tibeto-Burman group of the Han-Tibetan language family. Their former written script, based on the Latin alphabet, was reformed and standardized in 1957.   Before Liberation most Lahus were polytheistic in religious faith.   A minority were Mahayana Buddhists, Catholics or Protestants.

The Lahus possibly originated from an ethnic group

known as the Kunmings, who were reportedly roaming as
early as 2,000 years ago, in the time of the Western Han,
in the area of Erhai in Western Yunnan. From the 8th
century onwards, the Lahus were forced by circumstances
to move southward until they came to live in the area
where they now reside.

Their principal occupation is agriculture. They had
a feudal landlord economy before Liberation in some
areas, but in other places they still retained traces of their
earlier primitive communal system.

The Lahu men wear collarless jackets, wide-legged
trousers and black turbans; the women, long gowns with
silver ornaments on their collars and fronts. The wom-
en's headdress (as long as four metres in length) hang to
their waists. Their houses are built of bamboo.

In music, their dance movements are marked by
simple foot stamping and body swaying. They have their
own unique reed pipe wind instruments and three-string
plucked instruments.

The Naxis. These people have a population of 245,154
distributed in the Lijiang Naxi Autonomous County and
Zhongdian and Weixi counties of Yunnan Province, as
well as in the county of Yanyuan of Sichuan Province. A
few also live in Mangkang County in Tibet. Their language belongs to the Yi branch of the Tibeto-Burman
group of the Han-Tibetan language family. It comprises
two dialects, east and west. Though they had two written
scripts, known as "Dongba" and "Geba", long before
Liberation, these never became very popular and most
Naxis used the written script of the Han people. After
Liberation a new written script with a Latin alphabet was
devised to replace Dongba and Geba. Before Liberation

the Naxis generally believed in the polytheist "Dongba" religion.

The Naxi people trace their origin to the Maoniu tribe that lived in the time of the Western Han. They moved southward in the 7th century, settling in the area of modern Lijiang, Weixi and Zhongdian. By the 13th century the Yuan Dynasty had instituted a local administration of government in Lijiang. The Naxis today engage in agriculture, animal husbandry and handicraft industries. Before Liberation they had a feudal landlord economy, with some vestiges of a matriarchal society in a few villages.

The Naxi men dress more or less as their Han compatriots do. The women wear big-sleeved, long and wide jackets and vests, pleated aprons and sheepskin capes, embroidered with symbolic constellations that represent life "under the canopy of the moon and stars".

The Jingpos. This nationality has a population of 93,008, who live in the Dehong Dai and Jingpo Autonomous Prefecture and in mixed communities with people of the Benglong, Lisu, Achang and Han nationalities in Yunnan Province. The Jingpo language belongs to the Jingpo branch of the Tibeto-Burman group of the Han-Tibetan language family. Though the Jingpo people have long had their own written script, it had a rather rudimentary form before Liberation. After Liberation it was developed and standardized, although it is still based on the old written script. Among the Jingpos there are a number of people who believe in Protestantism, Catholicism and Buddhism.

The Jingpo people trace their origins to a branch of the Xunchuan tribe that existed during the Tang Dynasty. In more recent years they have been known as "Shantou",

"Dashan" or "Xiaoshan" people. But they called themselves by the name of "Jingpo" or "Zaiwa", and after
Liberation they settled on the name "Jingpo". They
engage mainly in agriculture. They entered the stage of
class society before Liberation, but retained some traces
of the primitive communal society from which they
originated.

They are a hospitable people and like to drink wine.
They eat their food from a plantain leaf. The men wear
short black jackets, wide short-legged trousers, and black
or white turbans. They carry sabres with them when
they are away from home. The women wear short black
gowns, woollen leggings, and multi-coloured pleated
aprons. They also like to wear silver ornaments.

The Jingpos are good singers and dancers, often engaging in group dancing. Sometimes they will even gather
together by the hundred to sing and dance to the accompaniment of wooden drums. Their ballads are sweet and
simple in style.

The Blangs. This group has a population of 58,476,
most of whom live in close communities in the Xishuangbanna Dai Autonomous Prefecture of Yunnan Province.
The remainder live in Shuangjiang and Zhenkang
counties of the Lincang area and Lancang and Jingdong
counties of the Simao area in Yunnan. Their language
belongs to the Cambodian group of Southeast Asian languages. They have no written script. Most of them
believe in Hinayana Buddhism, although a few are Christians.

The Blangs used to call themselves either "Blang",
"Wu" or "Wenggong", but after Liberation they decided
to take the common name "Blang". Historical records

indicate that their ancestors were the "Purens", "Puzis", "Pumangs" and "Pus".

Good at growing tea, the Blangs mainly engage in agriculture. Those living in Lancang, Jingdong and Muo-jiang counties before Liberation had a feudal landlord economy, while those living in the area of Xishuangban-na maintained a primitive communal system.

The Blang men wear collarless short jackets, black baggy trousers, and black or white turbans. The older ones let their hair grow long and wind it on top of their heads. The women, like the Dais, wear short, tight, collarless jackets and black or floral skirts. They tie their hair in buns on top of their heads. Some wear silver earrings, necklaces and bracelets.

The Blangs often perform the "Sword Dance" and the "Circle Dance", the latter being very popular among young men and women. The "Jump Song" has special appeal to Blangs living in the area of Muojiang. They dance to the accompaniment of "elephant-foot" drums, gongs and small three-string plucked instruments.

The Achangs. This nationality has a population of 20,441, living in Longchuan and Lianghe counties in the Dehong Dai and Jingpo Autonomous Prefecture of Yun-nan Province. Their language belongs to the Yi branch of the Tibeto-Burman group within the Han-Tibetan language family. They have no written script. Many Achangs also use the spoken language of the Dais and of the Han people, and they use Han characters for writing. Their religious faith is Buddhism.

As early as 2,000 years ago, in the time of the West-ern Han, the forefathers of the Achangs lived in the area along the Jinsha, Lancang and Nujiang rivers in north-western Yunnan Province. By the 7th century an ethnic

group known as the Xunchuan had moved into the Nujiang River area. Through contacts with this ethnic
group and the Jingpos, Dais and Bais, the Achang nationality came into being.

Their principal occupation is agriculture, although
their handicraft industry is also fairly well developed.
They have a number of fine rice strains, including
"Haoangong", sometimes called the "king of rice". The
Achangs are particularly skilful craftsmen in wrought
iron and other metal work. Especially noteworthy are
the swords made by the Achangs of the Husa area since
500 years ago. These are beautiful and sharp, and some
can be bent like a band and tied around the waist. These
swords are quite popular among the people of various nationalities in Yunnan Province.

Many folk tales, ballads and legends have been handed down orally for many generations among the Achangs.
Using these, they often engage in antiphonal singing.

The Achang men wear plain-coloured jackets with
buttons down the front and black trousers. The women
wear black or blue hoods, skirts and long small-sleeved
gowns with buttons down the front. The young girls
put on trousers and wind their plaited hair around their
heads. On festive days they deck themselves out with an
assortment of silver ornaments.

The Pumis. This group has a population of 24,237,
mostly living in Lanping, Lijiang, Weixi and Yongsheng
counties and in the Ninglang Yi Autonomous County of
Yunnan Province. A few also live in the Muli Tibetan
and the Yanyuan Yi autonomous counties of Yunnan. The
Pumi language belongs to the Tibetan branch of the Tibeto-Burman group of the Han-Tibetan language family.
They have a written script using the Tibetan alphabet

system, but this is not widely used. Instead, most Pumis use the written characters of the Han people. Most of the pumi people believe in witchcraft; a few believe in Taoism and Lamaism.

The Pumis call themselves "Puyingmi", "Purimi" or "Peimi". They have also been known at various times in the past as "Xifan" or "Baju". At one time they were a nomadic people living on the border area between Qinghai, Gansu and Sichuan provinces. After the 13th century they moved to Ninglang. At first they lived by livestock breeding, but then they changed to agriculture with livestock breeding as a sideline. Their economy was feudal before Liberation, and even tribal in a few places.

The Pumi people eat corn, rice, wheat and *qingko* barley. A favourite food is *pipa* meat, composed of whole salted and spiced pigs.

The women wear big turbans, large-lapel gowns, long plaited skirts, and silver earrings and other ornaments. The men wear short gunny jackets and large trousers. They arm themselves with sabres when they go on journeys. On festive days the Pumis engage in horse racing, target shooting, wrestling, antiphonal singing and dancing.

The Nus. This group has a population of 23,166 mostly distributed in Bijiang, Fugong, Gongshan and Lanping counties in the Nujiang Lisu Autonomous Prefecture of Yunnan Province. A few live in Weixi County in the Diqing Tibetan Autonomous Prefecture. Their language belongs to the Tibeto-Burman group of the Han-Tibetan language family, and it has several distinct dialects. They have no written script of their own, but use the characters of the Han people. In the past they believed in animism. Some believed in Protestantism, Catholicism and Lamaism.

Calling themselves "Nusu", "Anu" and "Along", the Nus claim that they are the descendants of an ancient people who lived on the banks of the Nujiang and Lancang rivers. They engage in agriculture and hunting. Before Liberation they were already in the stage of feudal society, except for those living in Bijiang and Fugong, who still retained vestiges of their earlier primitive communal system.

The Nus live mainly on corn and buckwheat. Both the men and women like to drink wine. They wear gunny clothing. The women also wear coral, agate and shell chest ornaments and bands of split rattan around their heads, waists and ankles. The men wear long gunny gowns or shorts, and have sabres, crossbows and arrows strapped across their shoulders.

The poems and songs of the Nu people are rich in the flavour of life. Though most of these are composed as extemporaneous pieces to the accompaniment of *pipa*, mouth-harp, flute and reed pipe, they are perfect in the initial rendition because they follow a traditional rhythmic form. Their dances are vivid, rhythmic, and unconstrained.

The Benglongs. These people number 12,295. Most of them live in close communities in the area of Dehong and Lincang of Yunnan Province. Others live in Yingjiang, Ruili and Longchuan counties of Yunnan along with the Jingpos, Hans, Lisus, Vas and Dais. Their language belongs to the Mon-Khmer group of South Asian languages. They have no written language, and commonly use either the written language of the Han people or that of the Dais. They worship Hinayana Buddhism.

In the past, the Benglongs referred to themselves by various names, including "Benglong", "Ang", "Leng",

"Liang" or "Bulei". Their present name became the uni-versally accepted one only after Liberation. Their fore-fathers were an ethnic group known as the Pus, who lived in the area of Dehong near the Nujiang River in the 2nd and 3rd centuries B.C. As farmers, they are highly skilled in growing tea. Before Liberation they were under the rule of clan chiefs and mountain lords who sub-jected them to harsh exploitation over a long period of time. During this period they still retained traces of primitive communal society.

The Benglongs live in stilted bamboo houses. Rice, corn, and sweet potatoes constitute their primary diet. The men wear either black or white turbans, big earrings and silver necklaces. Their black and blue jackets are open on the right and their trousers are short and wide. The women generally cut their hair short, and wear black turbans, blue and black tight-fitting jackets and long skirts.

The folktales, short stories, proverbs, songs and poems of the Benglongs are many and varied. Their mu-sical instruments include "elephant-foot" drums, gongs, reed-pipe instruments, flutes and small-sized three-string instruments.

The Drungs. This group has a population of 4,682, most of whom live in the valley of the Drung River in the Gongshan Drung and Nu Autonomous County of Yunnan Province. Their spoken language belongs to the Tibeto-Burman group of the Han-Tibetan language family. They have no written language. Formerly, as animists, they worshipped the elements and believed in gods and spirits.

The Drung people were known in ancient times as the "Qius" or "Qiongs". They have long engaged in agri-culture, hunting and fishing. In pre-Liberation days, they owned and farmed their land collectively in clans. Their level of production was low, and they used iron, wood and stone implements and distribute their harvests equally. Economically they were at the stage of development when patriarchal clan communes began to disintegrate.

Both the men and women grow their hair long. It hangs over their shoulders and is cut short at the front just above the eyebrows and ears. Formerly, they only wrapped themselves with a piece gunny cloth. But now they wear clothes made of cotton. Their houses are built of bamboo or logs.

The Drungs are highly musical and have many traditional songs and dances. The only festival they celebrate is that for the New Year. At that time they engage in friendly visits between the various clans and dance.

The Jinos. This nationality has a population of 11,974, who live in close communities in the mountainous area of Jinoluoke, Jinghong County in Xishuangbanna, Yunnan Province. Their spoken language belongs to the Tibeto-Burman group of the Han-Tibetan language family, and they have no written language of their own. They generally use the written script of the Han people. They practise ancestor worship and believe in gods and spirits.

Though history provides no written record of the Jino people, popular legends show that they formerly were part of an ethnic group that lived in Puer, Muojiang and other northern parts of Yunnan. They eventually settled on a small mountain ridge named "Jiezhuo", a place now known as "Tebateqian", where many of them still live.

They engage mainly in agriculture, and are good at

growing tea. Before Liberation, their economy was that of a primitive society practising slash-and-burn cultivation. They divided the meat acquired from hunting equally, giving the hides to those who caught them. After Liberation, with one giant leap, they moved economically from primitive society to socialism.

The men among the Jino people generally wear jackets with buttons down the front; the women wear red-bordered black skirts made on primitive weaving machines. They make many things of bamboo, including chopsticks, bowls, buckets and other daily utensils. They also use bamboo for building their houses.

They celebrate the New Year, known as "Temaoqie", by conducting sacrificial ceremonies to stave off scourges and to express their wishes for a good harvest.

The Miaos. These people number 5,030,897. About 54 per cent of them live in Guizhou Province; 17 per cent in Yunnan Province; 16 per cent in Hunan Province,. and the rest in Guangxi, Sichuan and Guangdong. Their language belongs to the Miao-Yao group of the Han-Tibetan language family. It consists of three dialects. They generally also use the Han language. A written script was designed for them in 1956. This is based on the Latin alphabet. In the past they believed in gods and spirits.

Depending on which local dialect is used, the Miaos call themselves "Guoxiong", "Mo" or "Meng". In different localities they are also named "long-skirt Miaos", "short-skirt Miaos", "highland Miaos" and "eight-stockade Miaos". History shows that as early as 2,000 years ago, during the Qin and Han dynasties, their predecessors lived in close communities in the area of Wuxi (five streams), which is in present-day western Hunan and

eastern Guizhou provinces.   Later they moved westward,
in succession, to gradually settle where they are now.

The Miao people are highly musical and produce fine
music and light-hearted songs.   Their dances are accompanied by reed-pipe instruments. They often hold a
"Dancing Party", a great mass celebration in the summer.
The participants often number several thousand and may
reach as many as 10,000.

Drawnwork, embroidery, batik printing, papercuts
and hand-woven patterned work by the Miao people are
beautiful and highly artistic.   Their batik printing has a
history of more than 1,000 years, and they have developed ways of doing this in multiple colours since Liberation.

They have a wide variety of traditional costumes.
The men grow their hair long, wear turbans, collarless
shirts and loose-fitting trousers, and tie sashes around
their waists.   The women wear their hair in buns, have
turbans on their heads and have floral sashes at their
waists.   They also wear bracelets, earrings and necklaces.

The Miao New Year is traditionally celebrated in
late autumn or early winter.   The festivities include a
"drum dance", bull fights, horse racing and dances to the
accompaniment of reed-pipe instruments.

The Bouyeis. This group has a population of
2,120,469, mostly living in close communities in the Qian-
nan Bouyei and Miao Autonomous Prefecture and the
area of Xingyi and Anshun in Guizhou Province.   A
small number of Bouyeis also live in the Qiandong Miao
and Dong Autonomous Prefecture of Guizhou.   Their
language belongs to the Zhuang-Dai branch of Zhuang-
Dong group of the Han-Tibetan language family.   A written script was designed after Liberation on the basis of
the Latin alphabet.   In the old days it was common

among the Bouyei people to believe in gods and spirits and to practise ancestor worship.

In the past they called themselves "Bouyei", "Bou-yai" or "Bouzhong", but after Liberation they settled on the name "Bouyei". They engage mainly in agriculture. Their houses, built generally on the sides of hills, have two storeys in the front and one storey at the back in accordance with the topography. These are known as "half-storeyed houses".

The Bouyei people like to wear black, blue and white clothes. The men wear blue or blue and white checked scarves on their heads, short jackets and long trousers. The women wear short jackets and trousers mounted with floral borders. They also wear hand-woven patterned scarves and short embroidered aprons of fine design. They twine their hair in long plaits on top of their heads.

The arts and handicrafts of the Bouyeis are well known for their high artistic level. Their batik works and embroidery are beautiful in design. Their homespun "Zhongjia cloth", straw mats and bamboo hats are in-genious in workmanship. The Bouyeis also have pro-duced a rich array of legends, stories, songs, poems, and folk tales. Some of their folk songs, based on themes that describe labour and love, are sung in antiphonal style by individuals and choruses. Song feasts among these people sometimes last for five or six days. Their tradi-tional festivals are celebrated on the third day of the third lunar month and the sixth day of the sixth month.

The Dongs. This nationality has a population of 1,425,100. They live in Guizhou and Hunan provinces and the Guangxi Zhuang Autonomous Region. The majority of the Dongs live in close communities in the Qiandong Miao and Dong Autonomous Prefecture of Guizhou Province. Their language belongs to the Zhuang-Dong group of the Han-Tibetan language family. They use the written script of the Han people. A written Dong script was created in 1958 using the Latin alphabet. They formerly practised ancestor worship and believed in gods and spirits, especially the "holy mother".

During the Qin and Han dynasties, the Dongs, who originated from an ethnic group called the Luoyue, lived in close communities in the area of Guangdong and Guangxi. They became known as Dongs only after Liberation. They engage mainly in agriculture, although they also do some lumbering.

Most of the houses of the Dong people are built of fir trees. They follow the topography of hills and face water. Most are two or three storeyed, but some have as many as four or five storeys. Towering at the centre of each village is a high multi-storeyed wooden structure with multi-angular eaves, that is used for village assemblies and recreational activities. The Dong people are also highly skilled at bridge construction. The most typical of their bridges are corridor-like "wind-rain" wooden bridges with multi-angular pagoda-like pavilions on them.

The Dongs produce a great variety of arts and handicrafts. Their embroideries are attractive and pleasing in style; their brocades and handkerchiefs are vivid, bright and beautiful in colour and are mounted with fine pictures. In addition they produce highly artistic articles of bamboo, wood and rattan, as well as carvings and papercuts.

The cultural life of the Dong people is rich and colourful, with many teams of singers giving visiting performances in the countryside. In fact, festive days are celebrated by the Dongs "in a land of poems and on a sea of songs". Their songs have a wide range of themes and follow strict rhyming patterns. They are often composed for responsive singing. Dances such as "Chiye", the Dragon Dance, the Lion Dance and dances to the accompaniment of reed-pipe instruments are those most often performed.

The Shuis. This group has a population of 286,487, who live in close communities in the Sandu Shui Autonomous County and in Libo, Dushan, Duyun, Rongjiang, Liping and Kaili counties in Guizhou Province. A small number also live in the northwest Guangxi Zhuang Autonomous Region. Their language belongs to the Dong-Shui branch of the Zhuang-Dong group of the Han-Tibetan language family. Their ancient written "Shui" script is used only in religion. It is common for the spoken language and written script of the Han people to be used in daily life. Formerly, the Shui people believed in polytheism.

Investigation shows that during the Qin and Han dynasties the Shui people were part of an ethnic group known as the Luoyue. They then lived in Lingnan and along the coast of southeast China. There are also historical records that indicate they lived in the border area of Hunan, Guizhou and Guangxi, at a place then known as Xidong, during the Sui and Tang dynasties.

Today they engage mainly in agriculture, cultivating rice, corn, barley and wheat. Glutinous rice, pickled vegetable, hot peppers, salted fish and meat, white spirits and rice wine are among their favourite foods. The traditional costumes of both the men and the women are either black or blue. Their houses are built in one or two storeys, but most in two with their cattle penned on the ground floor.

The arts and folk literature of the Shui people include folk tales, ballads and dances. Their folk songs usually have two melodies, one for daily use and the other for special occasions such as weddings, funerals and village feasts. The "Dragon Boat Festival" is a grand festival celebrated by the Shui people. On the days of this festival, the men and women put on their holiday best, sing, dance, engage in horse racing and visit relatives and friends.

The Gelos. This nationality has a population of 53,802 distributed in more than 20 counties of west Guizhou Province. A small number also live in Longlin County in Guangxi and in Wenshan County in Yunnan. Their language belongs to the Miao-Yao group of the Han-Tibetan language family. There are great differences among its local dialects. They have no written script of their own, and generally use the Han written script.

The Gelos trace their ancestry to an ethnic group named Laos that appear in the records of the Wei and Jin dynasties (3rd and 4th centuries). The ancient Laos led a settled life, engaging in agriculture in Guizhou Province. In the Tang and Song dynasties there are written records about them, and by the Ming Dynasty they were often mentioned in history books.

The Gelos live among the Hans, Miaos, Yis and Bouyeis, and they have adopted most of the foods, clothing, housing styles, wedding customs, birthday celebrations and other festive activities of their neighbours. But, in some respects, they still retain features characteristic of their own. Gelo women wear three-sectioned gathered skirts and hook-pointed shoes. Their sleeveless jackets,

short in front and long at the back, are embroidered with
fish-scale designs. Their hair is done up in buns bound
with long pieces of cloth and adorned with sea-shells.
There are also some Gelo women who like to have their
hair wrapped in a flowered handkerchief and to wear
silver beads on their foreheads.

(4) CENTRAL SOUTH AND SOUTHEAST CHINA: ZHUANG, YAO, MULAM, MAONAN, JING, TUJIA, LI, SHE AND GAOSHAN.

The Zhuangs. This nationality has a population of
13,378,162, making it the largest of the 55 minority nationalities in China. Over 90 percent of the Zhuangs live
in the Guangxi Zhuang Autonomous Region. A small
number also live in Yunnan, Hunan and Guangdong
provinces.

The Zhuangs originally were part of an ancient
ethnic group named the Yues. Before the Qin Dynasty
they lived over a wide area south of the middle and lower
reaches of the Changjiang River. Their language belongs
to the Zhuang-Dai branch of the Zhuang-Dong group of
the Han-Tibetan language family. The written language
of the Han people serves as their script. A new written
script was designed in 1955 using the Latin alphabet.

The Zhuang people generally engage in agriculture,
growing rice, corn, sugar-cane, tea, peanuts, tea-oil trees,
tung oil trees and bast fibres. Characteristic of their
splendid culture are their bronze drums and fine brocades.
The drums have a history of more than 2,000 years. The
ancient ones were used for military, worship and recreational activities. They are covered with exquisite pictures
and produce resonnant sounds. The Zhuangs also produc-

ed the Flower Hill cliff fresco, located in Ningming County of Guangxi. This ancient drawing was done with hematite powder on a cliff face of limestone. Altogether 135 metres long, it depicts more than 1,300 lifelike images of people and pictures of animals. The Zhuang brocades are famous for their exquisite and unique designs.

The songs of the Zhuangs are quite fine, and often improvised on the spot. The verses often contain metaphors, riddles and questions. They are sung during productive labour, at wedding celebrations and during other festive activities. With the coming of spring and during the fall each year, antiphonal mass singing parties are held.

Rice constitutes the main food of the Zhuang people. Salted fish and pickled meats are also served at meals, particularly for guests and friends. Their clothing is usually black in colour. The men wear black turbans and short jackets with buttons down the front. The women wear earrings, silver hair pins and necklaces. They trim their blouses and trousers with lace, and tie small aprons around their waists. The sacrificial festival and the New Year festival (lasting for 10 days after the first day of the 12th month of the lunar year) are happy occasions that they celebrate on a grand scale.

The Yaos. This group has a population of 1,402,676 living in Hunan, Yunnan, Guizhou and Guangdong provinces, as well as in the Guangxi Zhuang Autonomous Region, where over 70 per cent live. Their language belongs to the Miao-Yao group of the Han-Tibetan language family. They have no written language and generally use that of the Han people.

During the Qin and Han dynasties, the Yao people were part of an ethnic group known as the "Wuling tribe of Changsha". They were called "Moyaos" during the Sui and Tang dynasties, and "Yaos" after the Song Dynasty.

The Yao people engage mainly in agriculture and forestry. The men are good at hunting; the women do exceptionally fine drawnwork and embroidery. Before Liberation, because of the uneven development of the social economy, most of the Yao people remained at the stage of feudalism, while retaining some vestiges of their earlier primitive communal economy.

Their clothing is usually black and blue in colour. The men wear short jackets and short trousers. They grow their hair long and tie it on top of their heads. The women dress in striped short jackets and straight skirts. Both the men and women wear leggings, necklaces and black or blue turbans.

Rice is their main food. They also like glutinous rice and other foods eaten by the Han people who live nearby. They especially like hot pepper.

On festive days both the men and women like to sing songs. Their musical instruments include reed-pipes, "monkey" drums, bronze drums, flutes and vertical bamboo flutes. The Hunters' Dance, Bronze Drum Dance and Monkey Drum Dance are among the dances they traditionally perform.

The Mulams. This group has a population of 90,426, who live in the Guangxi Zhuang Autonomous Region. Most of them live in close communities in Luocheng County and nearby places in the region. Their language belongs to the Shui branch of the Zhuang-Dong group of the Han-Tibetan language family. Most of them know the Han language and use the Han written script since they have no written language of their own. A small number believe in Buddhism.

The Mulams were called "Laos" during the Jin Dynasty, and "Lings" during the Tang and Song dynasties. But in more recent times they have been known as Mulams. Most of them engage in agriculture, and some in coal mining and sulphur mining. The women are adept at apron and girdle plaiting.

They generally follow traditional styles in terms of housing, clothing and food, but many of the Mulams, because they have lived among the Han and Zhuang people, now follow the ways of their Han and Zhuang compatriots. Rice, corn and tubers constitute their main foods, and most Mulams dress in dark blue. In the past their clothes were homespun.

The Mulams enjoy singing and acting in theatricals. Their game "Zoupo" (meaning "walking on a slope") is a social activity highly regarded by young people.

The Maonans. This nationality has a population of 38,135, living in Huanjiang, Hechi, Nandan and Yishan in the northern part of the Guangxi Zhuang Autonomous Region. Their largest community, over 70 percent of all Maonans, is in the Xianan People's Commune of Huanjiang County, known as the "land of the Maonans". Their language belongs to the Shui branch of the Zhuang-Dong group of the Han-Tibetan language family. Almost every Maonan can speak the language of the Hans and the Zhuangs, and they use the written script of the Han people.

The Maonan people call themselves "Ahnan", which means coming from the place "Nan". Their ancestors came from an ethnic group known as the Baiyues.

The Maonans engage mainly in agriculture and beef cattle raising. Their neighbours often say that they are living in a "land of beef cattle". Their bamboo hats are highly valued, particularly their flower-bamboo hats that are plaited with bamboo strips. Maonan villages are generally built at the foot of a hill, and their houses have two storeys. The people live on the upper floor and cattle on the ground floor.

The Maonan people have always expressed their feelings with singing, composing impromptu songs to fit any occasion. Antiphonal singing is popular among young courting couples.

The Jings. These people number 11,995, who live in close communities in the autonomous county of Dongxing in the Guangxi Zhuang Autonomous Region. The off-coast islands of Wanwei, Wushan and Shanxin of this county are known as the "three islands of the Jings". At one time they had a spoken and a rather crude written language of their own, but because of long contacts with the Han people they have come to use the spoken and written script of the Hans. Many Jings believe in Buddhism and Taoism, and a small number in Catholicism.

Folklore and some written records show that the Jing people began to move to Dongxing from such places as Do Son in Viet Nam after the 15th century. Since then, they have been engaged in fishing, agriculture and salt refining. They ventured only into shallow waters before Liberation, but now engage in deep-water fishing and pearl cultivation.

Their traditional costumes are beautiful but plain in style. The women dress in narrow-sleeved, tight-fitting short jackets with buttons down the front, and in long and wide trousers. They also like to wear earrings. A few of the older ones still follow the traditional practice of dyeing their teeth black and wearing anvil-shaped hair buns. The men's jackets hang down to their knees and are narrow-sleeved. The men also wear sashes tied at the waist. The Jings live in low houses, in which they sit on the floor.

The Jings are musical and have a special single-stringed instrument of their own. On the day when people turn out at village meetings to worship their ancestors and express their wishes for a good harvest, "hamei" (singers) are invited to sing songs.

The Tujias. This nationality has a population of 2,832,743, living in the mountainous area that separates Hunan and Hubei provinces. Their language belongs to the Tibeto-Burman group of the Han-Tibetan language family, and they have no written language of their own. They commonly use Han characters for writing. A certain number of Tujias also know the language of the Miao people.

The Tujias take pride in calling themselves "Bizika" (meaning "natives") and calling the Han people "Kejia" (meaning "guests"). Historical records show that 2,000 years ago they settled in present-day western Hunan and Hubei. Together with other minorities they were then known as "tribes of Wuling". They took the name "Tuding" in the 10th century.

The Tujias engage mainly in agriculture, though they also do fishing and hunting, and have sideline industries in embroidery, weaving, knitting and plaiting. Their floral bed covers and scarves are beautifully and meticulously woven by the young women.

The Tujias have many folk songs, ballads and dances. The Arm-Swinging Dance is one of their most popular dances. With a strong national flavour, vivid and full of life, this ancient dance depicts scenes in which people go hunting, fight battles, engage in agriculture and participate in feasts. When this dance is held in the spring, as many as 10,000 people may join in. The folk songs have subjects related to love, battles, productive labour and pouring out of grievances. Almost every Tujia can compose or sing a song impromptu. The Tujia area is therefore known as the "land of songs".

The Lis. This group has a population of 817,562, living in Guangdong Province, mainly in the Hainan Li and Miao Autonomous Prefecture of Hainan Island. Their language belongs to the Zhuang-Dong group of the Han-Tibetan language family. A written script was designed for them in 1957. It is based on the Latin alphabet. Formerly they believed in ghosts and spirits and practised ancestor worship.

The Li people, as early as the Qin and Han dynasties, were a branch the ethnic group called Luoyue. They moved to Hainan Island from Guangdong and Guangxi. They have been known as the Li nationality since the Tang and Song dynasties.

The Lis engage mainly in agriculture. The Li women are skilled in weaving, especially with cotton. As early as in the Song Dynasty they were already well known for their brocades and bed sheets. Before Liberation they had a feudal landlord economy, with some vestiges of primitive communal society in a few Li villages.

The Lis generally live together in large families in traditional cylindrical houses. The women wear buttonless short jackets and straight skirts. Some have sweater-like jackets. They pin their hair in buns at the back of the heads with bone hairpins. They also wear embroidered scarves, earrings, necklaces and bracelets. The men grow their hair long and coil it over their foreheads or at the back of their heads. Their jackets have buttons down the front and are without collars.

The Lis are quite musical and have created a wealth of folk literature. Their folk songs have many melodies, some beautiful in unburdening feelings and some excited and high in spirits.

The Shes. This group has a population of 368,832, living in the mountainous areas of Fujian, Zhejiang, Jiangxi, Guangdong and Anhui provinces. Most of them live in Fujian and Zhejiang. Their oral language belongs to the Han-Tibetan language family, and they use the written language of the Han people. Formerly they practised ancestor worship and believed in gods and spirits.

Written records of late Song and early Yuan dynasties show that they have been known as Shes since that time (late 13th century). They popularly believe that Pheonix Mountain in Chaozhou, Guangdong Province, was the original home of their ancestors. Later, because of ruthless oppression by the ruling class, they were forced to go into hiding deep in the mountains and forests. Thus, to show that their ancestors were not indigenous people but people who had moved from other places, they call themselves "guest families in the mountains".

Living halfway up the mountains, the Shes engage mainly in agriculture, growing rice and sweet potatoes on terraced land. They also cultivate trees and tea. The Shes are quite hardworking, particularly the women who not only shoulder heavy family chores but also take part in field work throughout the year.

The women wear clothes that are characteristic of their nationality, with collars, sleeves and right fronts of the garments trimmed in lace. They tie colour bands around their waists. They also have beautiful designs of animals, birds, grass and flowers on their clothes. Their hair is placed in spirals or coils on top of their heads and graced with red floss.

The She people have produced many good singers. For centuries they have engaged in antiphonal singing. They often sing antiphonally when they work in the mountains, when they rest at home and when young men and women court each other.

The Gaoshans. This nationality totals 300,000. They make their homes chiefly in the mountainous areas of Taiwan, but they are also found on the plains, along the coast and on Lanyu Island. As the earliest inhabitants of Taiwan, the Gaoshans formerly lived in all parts of the island. Later, when the Japanese occupied Taiwan, they were forced to move into the mountains. They did not become known as Gaoshans until 1945, after the Japanese surrender. A number of Gaoshan people are also found on the mainland in Fujian Province and in the cities of Shanghai, Beijing and Wuhan. The Gaoshan language belongs to the Indonesian group of Malayo-Polynesian language family. It has no written form.

The Gaoshan people are mainly engaged in agriculture. They grow rice, millet and sweet potatoes. They also engage in hunting and fishing, and go in for weaving, knitting, plaiting and carving. Their carvings of snake-bodied images are highly valued. Over a long period of time they have worked with the Han people to reclaim the land of Taiwan.

The communities in which the Gaoshan people live are called "Shes". They usually comprise 60 to 70 households, although the largest She has 500 to 600 households. The She chiefs are generally elected by the households, although a few obtain the rank by heredity. The chiefs mediate conflicts, sponsor worship activities and call meetings to discuss matters concerning the She.

The Gaoshans who live in different places have different customs, living habits, and dialects. They also wear different costumes. The men generally wear capes, vests, jackets, shorts, turbans and leggings. The women dress in sleeved or sleeveless short jackets, or blouses covering only one shoulder, aprons, skirts or trousers. Their collars, sleeves, scarves and aprons are usually embroidered in beautiful patterns. Animal bones and shells arranged in various shapes are their favourite ornaments.

On festive days the Gaoshans often celebrate with singing and dancing to the accompaniment of bamboo flutes, vertical bamboo flutes, mouth organs and bow-shaped lutes. The women also sing while they are pounding rice with pestles and doing other tasks.

4. THE POLICY TOWARDS NATIONALITIES AND ITS ACHIEVEMENTS

The First Chinese People's Political Consultative Conference, in 1949, included representatives of the minority nationalities. The delegates developed a Common Programme which, working as a temporary constitution, systcmatically set forth the new policy towards the many nationalities of China.

It stipulated that "all nationalities within the boundaries of the People's Republic of China are equal. They shall establish unity and mutual aid among themselves, and shall oppose imperialism and public enemies in their midst so that the People's Republic of China will become a big fraternal and co-operative family comprising all its nationalities. Greater nationalism and local nationalism shall be opposed. Actions involving discrimination, oppression and splitting the unity of the various nationalities shall be prohibited".

The Common Programme also stipulated that "regional autonomy shall be exercised in areas where national minorities are concentrated. . . . All national minorities shall have the freedom to develop their spoken and written languages, and to preserve or reform their traditions, customs and religious beliefs. The People's Government shall assist the broad masses of all national minorities to develop their political, economic, cultural and educational construction work".

The policy towards nationalities in the Common Programme embodied the basic principles of the People's Government for solving the national problem in our country. The policy was later incorporated in the Constitution of the People's Republic of China, adopted by the First Session of the First National People's Congress in 1954. As stated in the preamble and other relevant articles of the Constitution, the tasks that the country faced in its national work during the transitional period were: to consolidate the unity of the country and the unity of various nationalities in a common effort to build the big family of the motherland; to safeguard the right

of equality between the various nationalities and practise
regional national autonomy; and to help the national
minorities carry out social reforms and in their economic,
political and cultural development, so that they could all
go over to socialism.

The Communist Party and the government resolutely
carried out the policy towards nationalities as stipulated
in the Common Programme and the Constitution.   In
performing tasks with respect to the national problem in
the transitional period, they did gigantic work and made
great achievements.

(1) INSISTING ON NATIONAL UNITY AND EQUALITY BETWEEN NATIONALITIES

Reliance on national equality, opposition to national
oppression, persistance in national unity and opposition
to national splitting are fundamental principles of the
Chinese Communist Party and the People's Government
in relation to the national minorities in the country.

Shortly after the founding of the People's Republic
of China, the government, recognizing that there still
existed misunderstandings and discrimination resulting
from former policies of the reactionary ruling class, conducted a programme of general education on national
equality, unity, mutual help and friendship among the
various nationalities. The government also issued a series
of laws and decrees to protect the rights of national
minorities and to eliminate the influence of the former
system of national oppression from history.

From 1950 to 1952, four delegations were sent by the
Central People's Government to visit the national

The great unity of all nationalities in China.

Northwest China

Hui

Yugur

A veteran farmer of the Hui nationality observing the growth of paddy rice.

Old herdsman of the Kazak nationality playing the Dombira.

Uygur   Tajik    Kazak    Xibe

Peasants of the Uygur nationality gathering Hami melons.

Mongolian　　　**Manchu**　　　**Korean**　　　**Oroqen**

Mongolian herdsmen on the grasslands.

Song and dance of the Manchu nationality.

Hunters of the Oroqen nationality.

Tibetan

Yi

Southwest China

Dai

Naxi

People of the Yi nationality make wooden household utensils.

Water-Sprinkling Festival of the Dai nationality.

Tibetan children.

Reed-Pipe Dance of the Miao nationality.

Jingpo

Jino

Miao

Shui

Central South and Southeast China

Zhuang   Yao   Yi   Gaoshan

Zhuang brocade, a handicraft product of the Zhuang nationality.

minorities in various parts of the country, including the Southwest, Northwest, Central South, Northeast and Inner Mongolia. The delegations covered more than 70,000 kilometres during their journeys and came into contact with 2,380,000 people. They inforfed the local people about the new policy towards nationalities in the minority nationality areas. In the meantime, delegations were also organized by the various national minorities to visit Beijing and other places.

From 1949 to 1964, the Central People's Government also sent 13 delegations deep in the minority nationality areas to convey greetings to the people of the minority nationalities. Furthermore, during this time, 268 delegations of minority nationalities, including approximately 10,000 people, met leading personalities of the Party and government. By facilitating the relationship between the central authorities and people of the various nationalities, these contacts led to a mutual understanding and strengthening of friendship and unity between the people of various nationalities in the country.

In May 1951, the Central People's Government issued a directive that all signs, place names, tablet inscriptions and billboards carrying derogatory terms or showing discrimination against minority nationalities should either be changed or removed. Thus the city names of Dihua in Xinjiang and Guisui in Inner Mongolia were changed to Urumqi and Hohhot. The words mean "pastureland of charm" in the Uygur language and "green land" in the Mongolian language.

In 1952, the Central People's Government issued a "Decision on Protecting People of All National Minorities Living in Scattered Groups to Enjoy the Right of

Equality". It stipulated that all minority nationality people living in scattered groups have the right to employment, to the use of their spoken and written languages
in legal proceedings, and to preserve their customs and
religious beliefs.

In order to help the people of minority nationalities
in taking part in the management of state affairs and to
ensure their participation in government administration
at all levels, the National People's Congress adopted an
Electoral Law stipulating that each minority nationality
living in a compact community shall be represented at
the people's congress of that locality. According to this
law, when the total population of a minority nationality
living in a compact community or living in scattered
groups represents less than 10 per cent of the total
population in any locality, the number of inhabitants represented by each deputy from the minority nationality
may be less one half that represented by other deputies
to the people's congress of that locality. The law also states
that even a minority nationality with an exceptionally
small population shall have at least one deputy to the
local people's congress and the National People's Congress. The Electoral Law ensures that, among the number
of deputies to the people's congresses at all levels, the
proportion of representatives from the various minority
nationalities will generally exceed that of the rest of the
population or of a specific locality, so that generally every
minority nationality, including those with a small population is represented at the national and local people's congresses. Below is a table showing the number of deputies
of minority nationalities represented at past National
People's Congresses:

Number of Deputies of Minority Nationalities at National People's Congresses

Congress	Total number of deputies	Deputies of the minority nationalities		Number of minority national-ities represented
		Number	Percentage to the whole number of deputies	
1st	1226	178	14.5	30
2nd	1226	179	14.6	30
3rd	3040	372	12.2	54
4th	2885	270	9.4	54
5th	3497	381	10.9	54

Note: The number of deputies to the 5th National People's Congress was based on figures from the first session of that congress.

(2) SELF-GOVERNMENT OF NATIONAL AUTONOMOUS REGIONS

China is a unified, multi-national country that has long had political, economic and cultural ties between the various nationalities. Over the long course of history, the people of various nationalities have come to live in large mixed groups alongside small self-contained communities. An inseparable relationship was formed between them during the more than 100 years' struggle against imperialism. In light of this and Marxist principles on the national question, the Chinese Communist Party formulated its policy on national regional autonomy. Under this policy organs of regional self-government were established in areas where minority nationalities live in compact communities. These organs of self-government, apart from exercising the functions and powers of normal state organs, also exercise the functions and powers of self-government within the limits prescribed by the Constitution and state laws. Every autonomous region or area is an inalienable part of the People's Republic of China.

The policy with respect to regional national autonomy embraces the following aspects:

1) Organs of self-government of the various nationalities are formed in the main of personnel of the minority nationalities concerned, with a proper representation from other nationalities in the area where they live.

2) Organs of self-government of autonomous areas, in exercising their functions and powers, use one or several languages commonly used by the minority nationalities in the locality concerned.

3) In performing their duties, the organs of self-government give full consideration to the traditions, characteristics and customs of the minority nationalities.

4) By taking into consideration the characteristics of the minority nationalities living in the areas concerned, the organs of self-government enact specific autonomous regulations and local laws.

5) In managing financial matters, the organs of self-government in the national autonomous areas enjoy greater financial power than other local governments at the same level.

There are three types of national autonomous areas in China. One is founded on the basis of only one minority nationality, such as the Ningxia Hui Autonomous Region, the Yanbian Korean Autonomous Prefecture in Jilin Province and the Songtao Miao Autonomous County in Guizhou Province. The second type includes autonomous prefectures and counties formed around the minority nationality with the largest local population in an area where there are several minority nationalities exercising national autonomy at lower administrative levels. The Uygur nationality in Xinjiang, for example, is allied with more than 10 minority nationalities in autonomous prefectures and counties in the Xinjiang Uygur Autonomous Region. The third type is composed of autonomous areas formed jointly by several minority nationalities, such as the Haixi Mongolian, Tibetan and Kazak Autonomous Prefecture in Qinghai, and the Longsheng Autonomous County in Guangxi. In these autonomous areas the various minority nationalities, whether large in population or small, share administrative responsibilities.

Even before the founding of the People's Republic of China, a policy of regional national autonomy was carried out in the Liberated Areas. In 1947 the Inner Mongolia Autonomous Region was established, the earliest and largest autonomous region in China. After the founding of the People's Republic, the policy was introduced throughout the country. In 1952 the government promulgated the "Programme of the People's Republic of

China for Implementing Regional National Autonomy",
and by 1953, 47 national autonomous areas had been
established. By the end of 1958, regional autonomy was
in effect for over 90 per cent of the population in minority
areas.   Tibet, the last minority area liberated, formally
inaugurated the Tibet Autonomous Region in 1965. China
now has five autonomous regions at the provincial level,
29 autonomous prefectures, 72 autonomous counties and
three autonomous banners.

The five autonomous regions are the Inner Mongolia
Autonomous Region, the Ningxia Hui Autonomous Region,
the Xinjiang Uygur Autonomous Region, the Guangxi
Zhuang Autonomous Region and the Tibet Autonomous
Region. The 29 autonomous prefectures, 72 autonomous
counties and three autonomous banners are distributed
as follows:

Distribution of Autonomous Prefectures, Counties and Banners

Area	Autonomous Prefecture	Autonomous County (Banner)
Hebei Province	—	2
Inner Mongolia Autonomous Region	—	3
Liaoning Province	—	2
Jilin Province	1	2
Heilongjiang Province	—	1
Hubei Province	—	2

Area	Autonomous Prefecture	Autonomous County (Banner)
Hunan Province	1	4
Guangdong Province	1	3
Guangxi Zhuang Autonomous Region	—	8
Sichuan Province	3	2
Guizhou Province	2	9
Yunnan Province	8	19
Gansu Province	2	7
Qinghai Province	6	5
Xinjiang Uygur Autonomous Region	5	6

Experience over the past 30 or more years shows that the implementation of the principle of regional national autonomy has been of great advantage to China. It has facilitated a combination of centralized leadership and unity in the country, while guaranteeing the autonomy and equality of the various nationalities, thus combining the general line and policy of the country with the actual features of the minority nationality areas. It has also helped in promoting the prosperity and strength of the country and the growth of the various nationalities, effecting among the minority nationalities feelings of affection for both the unification of the motherland and for their own nationalities. In other words, the practice of regional national autonomy has enabled all nationalities to work together with one heart and make great progress in many fields.

(3) TRAINING CADRES OF THE MINORITY NATIONALITIES

The key to exercising regional national autonomy lies in training large numbers of minority nationality cadres. Before Liberation, great attention was given by the Chinese Communist Party to the training of large numbers of minority nationality cadres. From the 1920s to the eve of the founding of New China there were more than 48,000 cadres of various minority nationalities trained in the revolutionary base areas. Contributions were made by these people to the strengthening of unity between the various nationalities and to the struggle for the victory of the democratic revolution in China.

In November 1950, soon after the founding of New China, the government outlined a policy for training large numbers of minority nationality cadres. This involved the promotion and use of minority nationality cadres and the opening of various types of special training courses and schools for minority nationality cadres. In addition to the Central Institute for Nationalities, founded in Beijing in 1951, there were nine institutes for nationalities established in the Southwest, Northwest and Central South and other parts of the country.

Over the last 30 or more years large numbers of cadres of the minority nationalities have developed, including a fairly large number of scientific and technical personnel. Working in various departments of science, education, culture and art, the press, and medical and health work, both in the central government and in the minority areas, they have become a backbone working force. Some have even become top leaders. As statistics show, by 1978 there were nearly 800,000 minority nationality cadres, more than 80 times the number there were in 1949.

The Rising Number of Minority Nationality Cadres in the Country

Year	1951	1953	1957	1962	1964	1978
Absolute figures	61,452	134,894	238,838	301,827	346,056	834,076
Percentage	100	219.51	388.66	491.16	563.13	1357.28

(4) FREEDOM FOR MINORITY NATIONALITIES IN USING AND DEVELOPING THEIR SPOKEN AND WRITTEN LANGUAGES

The Constitution and other laws of China stipulate that the various nationalities have the right to use and develop their own spoken and written languages. The government not only respects the spoken and written languages of the minority nationalities but helps them to develop their own.

Soon after Liberation, different language courses were instituted at the Institutes for Nationalities and at nationality schools and institutes in the minority nationality areas. Many people were trained for scientific research, translation and the teaching of the minority nationality languages. In 1951, under the Commission of Cultural and Educational Affairs of the Government Administration Council, a Committee for Guiding the Research on Minority Nationality Languages was established. Its purpose was to organize and guide research on minority nationality languages, give aid to those minority nationalities who wished to develop written languages of their own and perfect the existing written languages. In 1956 the state organized a language investigation team that included more than 700 language experts to carry out a large-scale scientific investigation into the languages of 33 minority nationalities living in 16 provinces and autonomous regions of the country.

In line with a policy of following the "will and decision of the minority nationalities" in facilitating their development and prosperity, an effort was made to help the Zhuang, Yi, Bouyei, Miao, Dong, Hani, Lisu, Li, Va and Naxi peoples develop their own written scripts on the basis of the Latin alphabet. Moreover, on the basis of two different dialects in Xishuangbanna and Dehong, two schemes were mapped out for the Dai people to reform their written script. The Jingpo and Lahu peoples were assisted in improving their written scripts, and the Uygurs and the Kazaks were aided in developing new written scripts on the basis of Latin alphabet.

The government has specified that organs of self-government in the regions of national autonomy should use the respective spoken and written languages, and that the written languages of various nationalities should be used in the election of deputies to the people's congresses. It has also been specified that citizens of every nationality has the right to use their own spoken and written languages in legal proceedings, and that the common language in the minority nationality areas should be used for interrogation, announcement of court verdicts, notices, bulletins and other legal documents.

Respect is given to languages being used by the minority nationalities in daily life, productive labour, correspondence and social contacts. These languages are also used in minority area schools and in local news releases, broadcasts and publishing work. The languages of the minority nationalities are used in books, newspapers and magazines published by central publishing departments and publishers in the autonomous areas. At the present time Mongolian, Tibetan, Uygur, Kazak and Korean are used everyday by the Central People's Broadcasting Station in programmes beamed to the minority nationality areas. Radio programmes are also produced with one or several minority nationality languages by regional and prefectural broadcasting stations in Inner Mongolia, Xinjiang, Jilin, Heilongjiang, Yunnan, Qinghai, Sichuan and Gansu provinces.

(5) RESPECT FOR THE TRADITIONS AND CUSTOMS OF THE MINORITY NATIONALITIES

The government takes great care to accord the proper respect to the traditions and customs of the minority nationalities, and assigns persons to do education work on this among the population as a whole. Serious offences against the traditions and customs of minority nationalities may be punished by a sentence of two years' imprisonment or other forms of custody as stipulated by the penal code.

The government has also adopted various measures to protect the traditions and customs of the minority nationalities. For example, leave is regularly provided for the festival days of the minority nationalities. Pig raising is discouraged among those minority nationalities that have traditions against eating pork, and workers and cadres of minority nationalities that believe in Islamism, such as the Huis, Uygurs and Kazaks, are provided with special meals at their places of work or given subsidies allowing them to have their meals at nearby Islamic restaurants. Special arrangements are also made for the production and supply of specific utensils and articles needed by the various national minorities. No interference or compulsion is permitted in regard to the preservation or reformation of legitimate traditions and customs by the people of the various nationalities.

Since Liberation, many of the old customs and traditions that benefit production and prosperity have been further developed. Take, for example, the Mongolian traditional festival called the Nadam Fair, the Corban of the Uygurs, the Ongkor (Harvest) Festival of the Tibetan people, the Water-Sprinkling Festival of the Dais, the Torchlight Festival of the Yis and the "Eighth of the Fourth Month" Festival of the Miaos. These have become days for strengthening national unity and days on which people carry out cultural and physical activities, exchange goods and exchange experiences in production. Before Liberation people used to discriminate against minority nationality people wearing their national costumes, but now people are at liberty to wear whatever costumes they wish.

As the political and cultural levels of the minority nationalities rise and their economy improves, they have taken steps to voluntarily give up some of the ancient customs and traditions that are emotionally and physically harmful. Among these practices are such customs as the slaughter of draft animals for purposes of worship; restrictions preventing men from transplanting rice seedlings and women from participation in ploughing; prohibitions against doing field work on special days; and the practice of polygamy, polyandry, early marriage and the giving of birth to a child outdoors. All these have been done away with by the peoples of various minority nationalities.

(6) RELIGIOUS FREEDOM FOR MINORITY NATIONALITIES

Religion has exerted a profound influence on the development of the economies and culture of the minority nationalities, and on the formation of their customs and traditions. The nationalities believing in Lamaism include the Tibetans, Mongolians, Tus and Yugurs. Those believing in Hinayana Buddhism are the Dais, Blangs, Benglongs and a section of the Vas. Those believing in Islamism are the Huis, Uygurs, Kazaks, Kirgizs, Tatars, Ozbeks, Tajiks, Dongxiangs, Salars and Bonans.

A section of the Miao and Yi people and a number of other minority nationalities living in western Yunnan Province believe in Christianity, the Russian nationality and a small section of the Owenkis believe in the Orthodox Eastern Church. Among the Drung, Nu, Va, Jingpo, Gaoshan and Oroqen people, and some other nationalities, there are still elements of nature worship and polytheism.

The Constitution stipulates that religious freedom is protected by the state. This is a democratic right enjoyed by all Chinese citizens. Every citizen has the right to believe or disbelieve in religion, and the freedom to practise their particular religious faith. This right is protected by the law.

The government therefore does not interfere in the normal religious life of the national minorities. These minorities are allowed to maintain their temples, mosques and churches, and the famous temples and monasteries are put under state protection, with the government being responsible for renovation and repair. The government maintains that religious activities should be conducted on the grounds of the temples, mosques and churches, and people who disbelieve in religion may not encroach upon these grounds to carry out propaganda about atheism. The criminal code of the state also stipulates that government employees who unlawfully deprive citizens of their freedom to conduct normal religious activities shall either be taken into custody or punished with a two-year prison sentence in serious cases.

The government's policy of religious freedom has helped to unite the broad masses of religious believers, especially the patriotic religious leaders, together with the people of the whole country in building socialism.

(7) ASSISTANCE TO ALL MINORITY NATIONALITIES IN THEIR ECONOMIC AND CULTURAL DEVELOPMENT

Agriculture and animal husbandry in the areas of the minority nationalities developed at a snail's pace in old China, owing to the discriminatory policies pursued by the ruling class. Industrial enterprises were almost nonexistent except for a few handicraft industries. After the founding of New China, the government took steps to eliminate the *de facto* inequality between the various nationalities by helping them to develop their economies and culture. From October 1949 onwards many measures and policies were adopted by the government in the areas of finance, trade, culture, education and public health in order to help the minority nationalities.

The people's government, in the early post-Liberation years, allotted to the national autonomous areas large sums of money in financial aid, including relief funds, loans and aid to facilitate the development of production, education and medical work. In minority nationality areas where there were grave shortages of the means of production, the government provided farm implements, draught animals, seeds and grain free of charge, and even exempted the minorities from taxes for a certain period of time. A wide network of supply and marketing co-operatives and state-owned trading agencies was established in the minority areas to supply the means of production and daily necessities and to purchase farm produce and sideline products at rational prices.

Every year the state increased its investment in capital construction in the areas of the minority nationalities. This is shown by the following chart of investments made by the state in capital construction in the autonomous areas of the minority nationalities:

Investments in Capital Construction in Autonomous Areas
(Unit: 100 million yuan)

1950-52	1953-57	1958-62	1963-65	1966-70	1971-75
5.60	40.78	119.93	45.06	90.06	152.12

Investments in Capital Construction in Autonomous Areas (Unit: 100 million yuan)

1976	1977	1978	1979	1980	1950-80
35.14	38.49	53.04	54.1	56.81	691.12

The Central People's Government also provided special and necessary allowances to the national autonomous areas. Special reserve funds were established for various autonomous regions, autonomous prefectures and autonomous counties, and a greater amount of provident budgetary funds and a wider range of financial expenditures were permitted for these areas than for other provinces and municipalities. Necessary subsidiary funds were allotted by the state every year to the autonomous areas for their development in economic construction. As a result of these policies and the development of socialist construction, the amount of reserve funds and financial income and expenditures in the various national autonomous areas increased every year. In 1978 alone, 342,930,000 yuan were allotted by the state to the national autonomous areas. In 1979, the total amount of financial income in various autonomous areas of the country came to 3,400 million yuan, a 6.8-fold increase over the 500 million yuan of 1952.

The following table shows the proportion of revenues and expenditures in the autonomous areas of minority nationalities throughout the country:

Revenues and Expenditures in Autonomous Areas

	Unit	1952	1957	1965	1979
Revenues	100 million yuan	5	11.5	19.4	34
Expend-itures	100 million yuan	4.4	12.4	23.4	88

	Unit	Index (%)			
		1952	1957	1965	1979
Revenues	100 million yuan	100	230	388	680
Expend-itures	100 million yuan	100	281.8	531.8	2,000

Note: The fiscal deficit in the budget of national autonomous areas was balanced by subsidies from the state.

Local authorities in the national autonomous areas were also given great autonomy in handling their revenues. In collecting state taxes, the organs of self-government in the national autonomous areas are permitted to make exceptions in special cases and reduce local taxes or exempt a national minority area from payment.

Besides the financial aid, large quantities of agricultural produce and industrial products, including a wide range of raw material, machinery, trucks and tractors have been allotted by the state to help in the development of the minority nationality areas. And many cadres, technicians, young people and workers have been sent by the state to help the minority nationalities in their economic and cultural construction.

A great effort has been made by the state to help in the development of culture, education and medical work in the minority areas. After Liberation, subsidiary funds for education and medical work were provided to the minority nationalities, and wide margins were given to students from minority nationalities in their entrance examinations for university study. Mobile medical teams were sent by the state to give free medical care in the minority nationality areas, and health and medical establishments were set up in many places for treatment, prevention of disease, the spreading of the knowledge on hygiene and the training of local medical workers.

Over the past 30 or more years, through this help by the state and the hard work of the people of various nationalities, significant changes have occurred in the minority areas. The following table shows the development of economy in the national autonomous areas from 1949 to 1980:

Considerable development has also occurred in education, culture, science and medical work in the minority nationality areas (For more details, see *Education and Science* and *Culture* in the "China Handbook Series"). Thus, under the guidance of the government's policy toward the national minorities, the people of these nationalities have worked hard to build socialism and brought about great changes in their lives.

But things have not always gone well since Liberation. For a certain period the policies of the government towards national minorities were disrupted and retarded by "leftist" errors. Starting in 1957, many minority nationality areas, like other places in the country, hurriedly went over to people's communes with the result that the relations of production did not accord with the development of the productive forces. This impeded the development of production. Moreover, by magnifying the class struggle, serious mistakes were committed that brought harm to the cadres and masses of the minority nationalities. The right of self-government for various minority nationalities also no longer received due respect in day-to-day work.

During the "cultural revolution" that lasted from 1966 to 1976, the two counter-revolutionary cliques headed by Lin Biao and Jiang Qing mounted frenzied attacks on various minority nationalities that impeded the course of their development and resulted in inestimable losses and consequences to construction in the minority nationality areas.

Only after smashing these two counter-revolutionary cliques did the country again take the right course in its relations toward the national minorities. By 1976 the country was again being steered in the right direction. All the correct policies towards nationalities that had been tested through practice before the "cultural revolution" were reiterated and enforced. As things stand today, China is forging ahead in its relations with the national minorities. The people of various nationalities are united as one in their struggle to eliminate vestiges of inequality left over from past history and in building a powerful, prosperous and modern socialist country.

Chapter   Three

OVERSEAS CHINESE

1. GENERAL ACCOUNT ABOUT OVERSEAS CHINESE

(1) THE MEANING OF OVERSEAS CHINESE, FOREIGN CITIZENS OF CHINESE ORIGIN, RELATIVES OF OVERSEAS CHINESE AND RETURNED OVERSEAS CHINESE

Before going into the history and relationships to China of the overseas Chinese, we need to clarify such terms as overseas Chinese, foreign citizens of Chinese origin, relatives of overseas Chinese and returned overseas Chinese.

Those who reside outside of China but still keep their Chinese citizenship are called overseas Chinese. They are, of course, a component part of the Chinese people and the Chinese nation. However, the following groups of people do not belong to the category known as the overseas Chinese: the inhabitants of Hong Kong and Macao; the Chinese who go abroad to visit their relatives, to take a tour, conduct an investigation or give lectures; Chinese students studying abroad; functionaries sent abroad by the Chinese government; and Chinese inhabitants living on the border who cross it frequently.

Foreign citizens of Chinese origin are those Chinese descendants who have adopted foreign citizenship. As they no longer have Chinese citizenship, they are no longer compatible in status with the overseas Chinese.

However, many of these people still have relatives in China.

Relatives of overseas Chinese include their spouses, other lineal dependents and collateral relatives who live on financial aid provided by overseas Chinese or who live with the other members of their family in China.

Returned overseas Chinese refers to persons who have come from abroad and settled in China.

(2) THE TOTAL NUMBER AND DISTRIBUTION OF THE OVERSEAS CHINESE

China is one of the countries that have the most nationals residing abroad. A saying that describes the number of overseas Chinese and their wide distribution goes like this: "Where the sea reaches, there can be found overseas Chinese."

Because of their wide distribution and the complex relationships regarding the citizenship of these Chinese descendants residing abroad, it is impossible to give precise statistics as to the number of such overseas Chinese. The available statistics relate only to Chinese descendants residing abroad. According to these statistics, there are more than 20 million such Chinese descendants. These consist of overseas Chinese and foreign citizens of Chinese origin. They reside mainly in the countries of Southeast Asia, such as Thailand, Malaysia, Indonesia, Viet Nam, Singapore, the Philippines and Burma. Some also live in the United States, Canada, Latin America, Oceania, Europe and Africa. And Chinese descendants can also be found in Japan, India, Pakistan and the Middle East.

The vast majority of overseas Chinese and foreign citizens of Chinese origin are of the Han nationality. Between 200,000 and 300,000 members of the Uygur and Kazak nationalities of China live in the Soviet Union, Saudi Arabia and Turkey, while about 100,000 members of the Tibetan nationality reside abroad, mainly in India. Furthermore, there are overseas Chinese and foreign citizens of China's Mongolian and Korean nationalities living abroad.

In China there are altogether more than 20 million relatives of overseas Chinese and returned overseas Chinese, distributed mainly in Guangdong, Fujian, Guangxi, Yunnan, Shandong, Zhejiang and Jiangsu. In the last 20 to 30 years a certain number of our compatriots in Hong Kong, Macao and Taiwan have gone to the United States, Southeast Asia and Europe to earn their living. Their relatives, who inhabit the hinterland of China, belong to the category of relatives of overseas Chinese or foreign citizens of Chinese origin.

(3) THE EMERGENCE AND DEVELOPMENT OF OVERSEAS CHINESE AND THE REASON FOR THEIR EMIGRATION

Historical Development China has had a long history of contacts with foreign countries. But in the early period, the contacts were established mainly in religion, culture and trade, and only a small number of people emigrated abroad. According to historical records, the emigration of Chinese people can be divided into the following periods:

In 540 (the sixth year of Datong reign of Emperor Wudi of the Liang Dynasty) overseas Chinese were to be found living in Japan. According to an investigation by the Japanese Minister of Finance, there were then 7,053 Chinese families in Japan.

In the book *Muruj adh-Dhahab (Meadows of Gold)* written by an Arabian author named al-Masudi (?-956), it is recorded that in 943 Chinese descendants were engaged in reclamation in Sumatera, Indonesia. It is also said that they went there to evade the chaos produced by the peasant uprising in the latter part of the Tang Dynasty, led by Huang Chao.

At the beginning of the Ming Dynasty (1368-1644) Zheng He made seven ocean voyages, reaching Southeast Asia, India, Persia and East Africa — altogether more than 30 countries. His adventures opened new sea routes for ocean-going vessels and built ties of friendship with other countries. According to the records in the *Famous Sights Across the Sea* written by Ma Huan, a man who travelled with Zheng He in these voyages, Chinese descendants emigrated to Java of Indonesia from Guangdong Province, and Zhangzhou and Quanzhou in Fujian Province. Zheng He's voyages in the 15th century actually provided favourable conditions for later emigration in large numbers.

During the 300 years from the beginning of the 16th century to the Opium War of 1840, Western colonialists invaded Asia and removed Chinese labourers along the coast to use as workers in other countries. The number of people who left China to settle down in other parts of Southeast Asia grew daily, totalling several hundred thousand to one million before 1840.

However, the largest emigration occurred during the period from the Opium War (1840) to around 1930. By 1911, there were nine million overseas Chinese throughout the world.

The above historical facts show that the emigration of Chinese people has a history of more than 1,400 years, if we count from the year 540 when Chinese residents were found in Japan; or at least more than 1,000 years, if we count from 943 when they were found in Indonesia.

Reasons Why Chinese People Went to Settle Abroad. The reasons why Chinese people settled abroad are as follows:

1) Refuge from chaos caused by war and from political persecution. At the end of the Tang, Southern Song and Ming dynasties, and after the failure of the Taiping Uprising, a number of Chinese people went abroad into exile. Also, after the failure of the First Revolutionary Civil War in 1927 and during the War of Resistance Against Japan a number of people went into exile or emigrated abroad.

2) The forced reduction of China into a semi-colonial and semi-feudal society, coupled with the poverty of the country and its people and the bankruptcy of its villages. Especially in Guangdong and Fujian provinces, most of the peasants who lacked arable land, could not endure cruel oppression and suppression and went abroad to earn their living.

3) The plundering of China by foreign powers. During the 16th and 17th centuries, the Western colonialists invaded Asia and, by every possible means, "recruited" Chinese labourers to work abroad as toilers. In the 19th century they inveigled Chinese labourers into working abroad as slaves with the excuse of recruiting them as "contracted labourers".

In 1860 the allied forces of France and Britain attacked and occupied Beijing, and the British government compelled the Qing government to sign the Convention of Peking (Beijing), which stipulated that those Chinese who were willing to go abroad to work either in British colonies or other places were allowed to make contracts with British citizens. Thus the sale of Chinese labourers came legalized. Following the suit, the United States and other countries also compelled the Qing government to sign similar treaties with them. As a result, such "contracted Chinese labourers", sent abroad at different times, reached several million. They had no freedom of person and were actually slaves, called coolies. The death rate on their voyages to other countries was high, about 15 to 30 per cent, sometimes even reaching 45 per cent. The modern history of overseas Chinese is history written in blood and tears by overseas Chinese who often emigrated against their will.

(4) CHARACTERISTICS OF THE OVERSEAS CHINESE

Due to their class background and experiences, overseas Chinese generally have the following major characteristics:

1) Most overseas Chinese are working people and peaceful emigrants, essentially different from colonialists. They went abroad destitute and with the hope of earning their living by their own hands and skill. They brought the friendship of the Chinese people with them to the peoples of other countries. They had no intentions of creating violence, plundering or invading other countries, as did the colonialists. Whether a region they were residing in was under colonialist occupation or had won independence from the colonialists, the overseas Chinese played an active role in the development of the region's economy.

2) The overseas Chinese have inherited the merits of the people of the Chinese nation, such as valiantness and industry, peace-loving natures, and unity and cooperation. They love their motherland and ancestral homes with profound national feelings. Many of them, although their families have lived abroad for generations, still keep to the traditions of Chinese culture and read and write the Chinese language. A large number of them long to return to their ancestral homes in their later years, much as falling leaves tend to settle on tree roots.

3) The long-term harmonious relationships between the overseas Chinese and the local people, together with their combined labour, have brought great contributions to the promotion of the local economy, culture and science. In Southeast Asia, the overseas Chinese have constantly supported the just struggles of the local people for national independence against the designs of the imperialists and colonialists.

(5) CONTRIBUTIONS TO REVOLUTIONARY STRUGGLES IN CHINA

In old China, many Chinese went abroad to earn their living because they could not endure the hard life in China or because they were subjected to political persecution. Having emigrated to foreign countries, they had to depend on others for a living and were often subjected to bullying, humiliation and persecution. The reactionary governments of old China, incompetent as they were, failed to protect the just rights and interests of the overseas Chinese. How these people wished for the emergence of an independent and prosperous China!

How they longed for China to help them overcome their
destiny as "overseas orphans" and change the destiny of
their relatives in China. They fully supported and took
an active part in the revolutionary struggles against imperialism and feudalism in China, and their efforts led
to great contributions.

The Revolution of 1911 During the bourgeois-
democratic Revolution of 1911, led by Dr. Sun Yat-sen
(1866-1925), overseas Chinese made significant contributions. Dr. Sun highly praised the heroic deeds they performed on behalf of the revolution, and he acclaimed the
overseas Chinese community as the "mother of revolution".

In 1894 Dr. Sun Yat-sen founded the *Xing Zhong
Hui* (Society for the Revival of China) in Honolulu. It
gained full support from overseas Chinese. Many of
them took an active part in its organization, and 78 per
cent of its members were overseas Chinese. In 1905 the
Xing Zhong Hui, Guang Fu Hui (Restoration League) and
Hua Xing Hui (China Revival League) merged to form
in Tokyo the *Tong Meng Hui* (Chinese Revolutionary
League), which set up branches in Southeast Asia, Europe
and America. The overseas Chinese also functioned as
the mainstay in this revolutionary organization.

The vast majority of overseas Chinese offered
financial assistance to the revolution. Most of the expenses spent for uprisings during the Revolution of 1911
were contributed by them. Statistics show that the
overseas Chinese contributed five to six million yuan in
1911 alone, an enormous sum at that time. In order to
contribute funds to save China, many overseas Chinese
risked bankruptcy of their families. Take, for example,
an overseas Chinese, Chen Chu'nan, in Singapore. He

contributed more than 100,000 yuan to help settle over 500 revolutionary soldiers in Singapore after the Hekou Uprising. As a result, he almost went bankrupt. After the failure of the Huanghuagang Uprising, the revolutionary party badly needed funds. Having accepted a suggestion put forward by Situ Meitang, the *Zhi Gong Tang* in Vancouver and other parts of Canada pawned three of its office houses for 100,000 U.S. dollars and handed this sum to Dr. Sun Yat-sen. Moreover, many labouring overseas Chinese contributed the money they had earned through hard labour to the revolution.

Quite a number of overseas Chinese patriots returned home to take part in uprisings. From 1895, the second year of the founding of the *Xing Zhong Hui*, to 1911, the year of launching the Wuchang Uprising which overthrew the Qing Dynasty, Dr. Sun Yat-sen led over 10 uprisings in which overseas Chinese were participants. The Huanghuagang Uprising of April 27, 1911, an event which shocked the world, was planned and prepared by Dr. Sun Yat-sen and Huang Xing in Malaya. More than 500 overseas Chinese participated in it. Of the 72 martyrs (actually 86 died) in this event, 29 were overseas Chinese. They had come from Malaysia, Singapore, Viet Nam, Burma, Indonesia, etc., and among them there were workers, clerks, teachers, journalists and missionaries. They all fought bravely and proved themselves to be fine sons and daughters of the Chinese nation.

The Period of the First Revolutionary Civil War. The vast majority of the overseas Chinese also gave strong support to the First Revolutionary Civil War that lasted from 1924 to 1927. During the Canton-Hong Kong Strike, held from June 1925 to October 1926, overseas Chinese contributed three million yuan, or half of the ex-

penses used in the strike. This, of course, was an important material factor in causing the strike to last so
long. Besides, the overseas Chinese made use of the
favourable conditions abroad to propagate the event so
as to win the support and sympathy of the international
media and of the labouring people of various countries.

In July 1926, the revolutionary forces started the
Northern Expedition, and the overseas Chinese in Indonesia, the Philippines, the United States and other
countries set up the "Society for Supporting the Northern
Expedition", the "League for National Salvation", etc.,
to support this event and to contribute to its activities.
After the failure of the First Revolutionary Civil War,
the patriotic overseas Chinese did their best to support
the revolutionary people in their struggles against the
Kuomintang reactionaries.

**The Period of the Anti-Japanese and National Salva-
tion Movement and the Eight Years of the War of Resistance Against Japan.** During the Anti-Japanese and
National Salvation Movement, from 1931 to 1937, and
during the War of Resistance Against Japan, between
1937 and 1945, overseas Chinese all over the world gave
their compatriots at home enormous support, both in
terms of morale and materials. The September 18th Incident and January 28th Incident of the Japanese im-
perialist invasion of China aroused the patriotic
enthusiasm of the mass of the overseas Chinese. They
collected relief funds for the country, held overseas Chinese rallies to send telegrams urging the authorities to
oppose Japan, boycotted Japanese goods and carried on
propaganda against the Japanese imperialists.

By the time the War of Resistance Against Japan
broke out on July 7, 1937, their patriotic movement was

in full swing. The overseas Chinese in various countries organized societies for relief collection, reinforcement associations against the enemy, and one after another contributed more money to the country by economizing on food and clothing. During the period from 1937 to the beginning of 1940, overseas Chinese contributed an average of 20 million yuan a month, which was one third of the monthly military expenditure at the time. Between October 1938 and December 1940, the General Association of Overseas Chinese in Southeast Asia for Collecting Relief Funds, led by Tan Kah Kee, and its branches in other places contributed 144.45 million yuan to aid those fighting the War of Resistance Against Japan. Including the sums they contributed in 1937 and 1941, the total amount they provided reached 200 to 300 million yuan. In addition to these relief funds, the General Association of Overseas Chinese in Southeast Asia for Collecting Relief Funds also bought bonds of national salvation from China and sent medicines and winter clothes to China.

During the eight years of the anti-Japanese war, the sum contributed by the overseas Chinese in the United States totalled more than 56 million U.S. dollars, while that contributed by overseas Chinese in Canada, Mexico, Cuba, Jamaica and other countries totalled more than 10 million U.S. dollars. Furthermore, overseas Chinese offered assistance in terms of manpower and materials. Many of them returned to China to participate actively in the war.

Answering a call put out by the General Association of Overseas Chinese in Southeast Asia, many overseas medical personnel and aviation volunteers came to China to serve the anti-Japanese cause. Nine groups of 3,600 overseas Chinese took part in transportation work on the Yunnan-Burma Highway. Their contribution helped to break the Japanese blockade. Moreover, a number of overseas Chinese went through blockades to Yan'an and other revolutionary base areas to join the Eighth Route Army, New Fourth Army, East River Column and other anti-Japanese army units. Meanwhile, overseas Chinese contributed a large amount of medicine, medical equipment and other materials, some of which even reached the Liberated Areas.

The Period of the War of Liberation. During the War of Liberation, which lasted from 1945 to 1949, the patriotic overseas Chinese were a component part of the broad united front of the Chinese people against the Kuomintang government headed by Chiang Kai-shek. They opposed U.S. imperialism which helped Chiang Kai-shek in the civil war.

In September 1946, the General Association of Overseas Chinese in Southeast Asia, headed by Tan Kah Kee, announced that they did not recognize the puppet national assembly, constitution and president, but supported the Communist Party of China and held that it was the Communist Party of China that could transform and save China. In October 1949 the People's Republic was founded, which the overseas Chinese had been dreaming of for so long. Filled with exultation, overseas Chinese were determined to participate in the building of New China.

(6) CONTRIBUTIONS TO CHINA'S CONSTRUCTION

The overseas Chinese have given various types of support to the economic construction of China.

Overseas Remittance Before Liberation in 1949, overseas Chinese provided much financial support to their families in China, and more than 80 per cent of the income of these families came from overseas remittances. However since Liberation, the reliance on overseas remittances has declined because family dependents and returned overseas Chinese now have more chances for employment. As for families that lack labour power, overseas remittances still are a primary source for their income. Besides, overseas remittances remain a normal source by which the state can obtain foreign exchange. Thus overseas Chinese play an active role in the economic construction of their ancestral hometowns.

Investment in China Made by Overseas Chinese. Since the end of the 19th century, overseas Chinese have successively invested in China. According to the incomplete statistics, 25,510 enterprises were set up between 1862 and 1949 by overseas Chinese who invested a total of 128 million U.S. dollars in such enterprises. Most of them were newly developed enterprises, such as factories, railways, highways, banks and municipal construction.

The first overseas Chinese to invest in China was Chen Qiyuan, who set up the Jichanglong Mechanical Reeling Mill in Nanhai County, Guangdong Province. Its products were sold in Europe and America. In 1892, Zhang Bishi, an overseas Chinese living in Indonesia, invested 3.5 million taels of silver to set up the Zhangyu Grape Wine-Making Company in Yantai of Shandong Province. At the beginning of the 20th century, two overseas Chinese brothers, Zhang Yaoxuan and Zhang Rongxuan in Indonesia, Chen Yixi in the United States and others collected funds to build railways in Guangdong. In 1916, two overseas Chinese brothers, Jian

Zhaonao and Jian Yujie, in Japan established the Nan-
yang Brothers Tobacco Company. In 1921, an overseas
Chinese named Huang Yizhu set up the Zhongnan Bank
in Shanghai. In the early 1930s, patriotic overseas Chinese invested funds to set up, in Shanghai, four big department stores named the Yongan, Xinxin, Xianshi and
Daxin stores.

Before Liberation the funds invested by overseas
Chinese were used to import modern industrial equipment and to train technical workers. This promoted the
development of China's national capitalist economy to
some extent and improved transportation and the people's living conditions in the native districts of the
overseas Chinese. However, most of the enterprises
invested in and run by overseas Chinese, like other national industries and commerce in China, failed under the
oppression of imperialism, feudalism and bureaucrat
capitalism.

After the founding of New China, the enthusiasm of
overseas Chinese for investing in China has risen. The
enterprises they have invested in include textiles,
chemicals, sugar refining, machinery, electrical appliances, hydropower stations, tinned food, fisheries, reclamation farms, travel services, cinemas and theatres.
These enterprises have played an active role in promoting production and construction in China, improving
the living conditions of the people and providing the returned overseas Chinese with more chance of employment. After the State Council approved, in 1980, special
investment policies and flexible measures for Guangdong
and Fujian provinces, more overseas Chinese and compatriots in Hong Kong and Macao have come to invest

funds for setting up enterprises to support China's socialist construction.

Contribution of Funds to Set Up Schools. Before the founding of New China, most of the schools in the native towns of overseas Chinese were aided with funds contributed by them. For instance, 90 per cent of the schools in Jinjian County of Fujian Province, consisting of four middle schools and more than 200 primary schools, received financial assistance from overseas Chinese.

Overseas Chinese Tan Kah Kee set a good example of supporting schooling in his motherland. Since 1913 he has contributed funds to set up primary, middle, vocational, and normal schools in his hometown. These go under the general name of Jimei Schools. In 1919 he offered his immovable property, a 7,000-acre rubber plantation and 1.5 million square feet of land, to the Jimei Schools as a school fund, enabling the schools to grow larger and larger. At the risk of losing all his family property, he established Xiamen University with his own money and bore all the school expenses. When his enterprises suffered economic losses, he sold his rubber plantation and capital stock in an attempt to keep the schools going. After the founding of New China, all the expenses of Jimei Schools and Xiamen University have been paid by the state, while funds still contributed by Tan Kah Kee have been used to enlarge the schools. His patriotic and home-loving deed in contributing funds for the setting up of schools has promoted culture and education in Fujian Province.

For 60 years Xiamen University has trained nearly 20,000 graduates and postgraduates, who are now working everywhere in China and in the world. A number of them have become outstanding scholars and technicians. Jicmei Schools have also trained thousands of graduates, and quite a number of them from the Jiemei Navigation School have become leaders in the field of navigation both at home and abroad. Tan's spirit has exerted a profound influence on many other overseas Chinese. In recent decades, it has become a common practice among overseas Chinese to make contributions for assisting schools in China.

During the period from 1948 to 1959, the number of primary and middle schools set up with funds provided by overseas Chinese increased to more than 2,000 in Guangdong and Fujian provinces. Zhejiang, Yunnan and Guangxi also have such schools. In recent years overseas Chinese have continued to make contributions to develop culture and education of their native places.

Developing Public Welfare. Overseas Chinese also have contributed funds for developing charities and public welfare. They have provided money to set up hospitals, repair bridges, pave roads and give relief to people in disaster areas. When a flood occurred in Tianjin in 1915 and when the Jinan Incident happened in 1928, overseas Chinese in Singapore contributed large sums in relief funds. During the War of Resistance Against Japan and after Japan's surrender, overseas Chinese in Thailand bought rice with money they collected, and sent it to the famine areas of Chaozhou and Shantou in Guangdong Province. With the founding of New China, more efforts were made by overseas Chinese to develop the public welfare of their hometowns. Thus, over the period of a century, numerous welfare and public utilities have been completed in China by overseas Chinese.

(7) SUPPORT OF NATIONAL INDEPENDENCE IN THEIR COUNTRIES OF RESIDENCE

The overseas Chinese have always stood on the side of the people in their struggles for independence and against the colonialists, imperialists and aggression. Many of them fought bravely, or even gave their lives, for the emancipation and happiness of the local people.

In the Philippines. During the period of more than 300 years from the 16th to the end of 19th centuries, when Spanish colonialists ruled over the Philippines, overseas Chinese joined the local people in staging many uprisings to oppose the Spanish colonialists. The attacks launched in 1574 by forces under the command of the "Hero on the Seas", who was an overseas Chinese named Lin Feng, and the assassination in 1594 of the Spanish governor in the Philippines by Pan Hewu, another overseas Chinese, inspired the early struggles of the Philippine people against the colonialists. To suppress the resistance of the overseas Chinese, Spanish colonialists slaughtered 50,000 of them between 1603 and 1639. In the war for the independence of the Philippines in 1896-1902, overseas Chinese collected funds for the revolution and joined the revolutionary forces to actively fight Spain and the United States. A well-known overseas Chinese named Liu Hengbo led 3,000 of his compatriots in the war and won many battles. Because of his glorious deeds, he was promoted to Brigadier by the first president of the Republic of the Philippines. He is today still praised as a "real hero fighting for the freedom of the Philippines". During the Pacific War, overseas Chinese organized themselves into an overseas Chinese detachment and fought the Japanese at the side of the Philippine people, coordinating their military operations with the Allied forces.

In Indonesia. For over 300 years of rule under the Dutch colonialists, overseas Chinese in Indonesia supported the people in their struggles against the Netherlands. They gave active support to the armed uprising of 1686-1706, which was led by the "Slave", Surapati. In October 1740, the Dutch colonialists precipitated the Angke River Massacre, slaughtering many overseas Chinese. They then organized themselves into an armed force of 15,000 people and fought battles against the Dutch in the areas of Tjirebon and Semarang. In 1772, an overseas Chinese called Luo Fangbo led thousands of his compatriots in mining gold and reclaiming wastelands in West Borneo. He organized his followers into an autonomous, self-defence organization, the Lanfang Company. United with the local people, this company waged a long struggle against the Dutch colonialists. In the Java War that lasted from 1825 to 1830, an uprising led by Diponegro, an Indonesian national hero, overseas Chinese made great contributions by supplying manpower, arms and ammunition. Later, in the Indonesian Nationalist Movement of the latter 19th century to the 1930s, and during the Pacific War, the overseas Chinese gave great support to the local Indonesian people in their struggles against aggression.

In Singapore and Malaysia. During the Second World War, overseas Chinese throughout the world fought bravely against the German, Italian and Japanese fascists along with the people of the Allied countries. At the time when the Japanese imperialists occupied much of Southeast Asia, overseas Chinese, together with the local people, resorted to various forms of struggle against Japan. In Singapore, they set up the General Mobilization Society Against the Enemy and organized overseas Chinese volunteers to fight Japan. In Malaysia, after the surrender of British troops to Japan, overseas Chinese and the local people organized the Malaya People's Army of Resistance to Japan, and fought a heroic and bitter struggle for three years and eight months until final victory.

In Viet Nam. Overseas Chinese fought shoulder to shoulder with the Vietnamese people during the occupation by France that began in 1858, especially in the years between 1873 and 1885 when the Black Flag Army, led by Liu Yongfu, fought together with the Vietnamese army to repeatedly defeat French units. After his return to China, many generals under Liu Yongfu's command remained in Viet Nam to resist France. At the beginning of the 20th century when Phan Boi Chau, a Vietnamese revolutionary, organized the Restoration Society, overseas Chinese gave great support to its struggle against France. In the people's revolutionary struggle of Viet Nam that was led by Ho Chi Minh after the 1920s, overseas Chinese also gave their full support and fought shoulder to shoulder with the Vietnamese. For more than 100 years of struggle against France, Japan and the United States, overseas Chinese fought bravely, making great sacrifices and contributions at the same time.

In Russia. During the great socialist October Revolution, thousands of labouring overseas Chinese participated in the Red Guards, guerrilla units and the Red Army, fighting bravely beside the people of Russia. At that time, combat units such as the Chinese Regiment and the Chinese Red International Column were part of the Red Army. Chinese soldiers in the Red Army were praised by Lenin for their fighting spirit and strict discipline; many of them won the Order of Lenin.

In Cuba. In 1868, when the war of independence against Spanish colonialist rule broke out in Cuba, overseas Chinese labourers fought shoulder to shoulder beside the Cuban people to the bitter end. They fought bravely and did not fear sacrifices. When they were captured, they behaved heroically and justly, unafraid of death. In memory of the Chinese martyrs who died in the war of independence, the Cuban people have erected in Havana Square a monument on which is engraved the praising words of General Gonzalo: "There is not a single deserter and not a single traitor among the Chinese in Cuba."

The peoples of the world will never forget the vast numbers of overseas Chinese who gave all-out support to their revolutionary struggles. And they will never forget the Chinese soldiers who fought bravely and shed blood together with their own worthy sons and daughters.

(8) CONTRIBUTIONS MADE BY OVERSEAS CHINESE TO THE ECONOMIC AND CULTURAL DEVELOPMENT OF THEIR RESIDENT COUNTRIES

Most overseas Chinese emigrated to their resident countries to work as labourers. For centuries they have made great contributions to the local economy and local culture through their hard labour, and knowledge of handicrafts and technology.

In Southeast Asia. In the early period of their emigration into Southeast Asia, the overseas Chinese brought with them comparatively advanced techniques of production in fields such as sericulture, silk-weaving, paper-making, and tea production. This promoted the development of the local economy. In many parts of Southeast Asia they reclaimed wasteland, built railways and highways, engaged in agriculture, industry, commerce and fishing, and constructed cities and towns.

As early as in 15th century, they began to settle in Tuban, Gresik, Surabaya and Palembang in Indonesia and in Malacca in Malaysia. This resulted in the early development of these cities and towns. Later, in 1619, overseas Chinese began to establish commercial and industrial enterprises in Batavia (Djakarta); in 1660 Wu Shangxian built a silver mine in Burma; in 1679 Yang Yandi and Chen Shangchuan began to develop commerce and industries in Bien Hoa and the Cholon region of south Viet Nam; in 1671 Mo Jiu set up enterprises in Ha Tien in south Viet Nam; in the mid-18th century Wu Yang began to develop industries in Songkhla in southern Thailand; and in 1776 Luo Fangbo began to set up enterprises in Pontianak in West Borneo and other places. In the period between the end of the 18th century and the beginning of the 19th century, overseas Chinese set up enterprises in Pinang, Singapore and Kuala Lumpur; in the beginning of the 20th century overseas Chinese were engaged in land reclamation in Sarawak. They turned remote, backward places into large cities and waste and sandy land into fertile fields. The completion of some major cities in Indonesia, Malaysia, Singapore and Viet Nam was also partly due to the efforts of the overseas Chinese labourers.

Many enterprises in Southeast Asia were first started by overseas Chinese, such as the Malaysian rubber industry by Chen Qixian, Tan Kah Kee, Lin Wenqing and others, the famous Fishery of Bagan Siapiapi in Indonisia, and the world-famous Deli Tobacco Plantation of Indonesia. The sugar refining industry in Java in Indonesia, the pepper plantations in Viet Nam and the tin mines in Malaysia were also developed by overseas Chinese.

There are a large number of traders and a small number of industrialists and businessmen among the overseas Chinese. The traders promote interchange between the local urban and rural economy and bring convenience to people's daily lives. Most overseas Chinese industrialists and businessmen are engaged in small and middle-sized industrial enterprises. In the developing countries of Southeast Asia, the industries and commerce owned by overseas Chinese are a component part of the national economy, and thus play a role in the local national economy.

The efforts made by overseas Chinese in developing Southeast Asia have been recognized in the West and by most of the local people. In the Rafles Museum of Singapore there is a bronze statue of an overseas Chinese, completed by a sculptor named Stirling. It has these words engraved on it: "The Chinese are well-known for their fortitude and hard work. Today's prosperity of Singapore, Pinang, Malacca and even the whole of Malaya has benefitted in no small way from the labour of the Chinese."

In America. During the early period of emigration, overseas Chinese in the United States and Canada built railways, reclaimed waste land, exploited mines, planted fruit trees and grew vegetables, while those living in Panama dug the Panama Canal. In Peru they made economic use of bird's droppings and in Cuba they planted sugar cane. Thus the overseas Chinese made great contributions to the economic development of the two American continents.

But after 1785, overseas Chinese in the Americas experienced nearly 200 years of hardships. When the western United States was being developed, there was need for an enormous amount of labour power, and a large number of Chinese were recruited to work there. They engaged in the hardest jobs, jobs which white people refused to do. They reclaimed 5.5 million acres of wasteland and turned it into fertile fields. In the 1830s, when the Central Pacific railway was under construction, they undertook the most difficult tasks on the project, and many of them died in this work. During the celebration of the centenary of the founding of the state of Nevada, in 1964, a monument to the overseas Chinese was erected at Virginia City. On that monument the inscription reads:

CHINESE IN NEVADA

This honors the heroism and hardihood of the thousands of Chinese who played a major role in the history of Nevada from across the Pacific. The Chinese came to California during the gold rush of '40s and on to the mountains and deserts of this state they built railroads, cut timber and performed countless humble tasks.

Sizeable Chinese communities grew up here, in Virginia City and other towns. Their contribution to the progress of the state in its first century will be forever remembered by all Nevadans.

Nevada Centennial Marker No. 20

The state governor declared the 24th of October each year as a day to pay tribute to the Chinese pioneers.

From 1880 to 1885 more than 25,000 Chinese participated in building the transcontinental Canadian Pacific through Canada. The completion of this railway played an important part in the economic development and prosperity of Canada. The construction of this railway, which is twice the length of the railway they built in the United States, was much more difficult. Several hundred Chinese labourers gave their lives during the building. The Canadian authorities have said it is obvious that without the amazing efforts of the overseas Chinese, the railway could not have been completed in the year 1885.

In Panama, the overseas Chinese took part in the project to cut the Panama Canal from 1872 to 1919, and constructed a railway there in 1850. Their contributions to these two projects are also indelible.

In Russia. During the period from the end of the 19th century to the First World War, Russia recruited 200,000 Chinese labourers to work in Russia. The Chinese labourers worked in many places, such as on the worksite of the Murmansk Railway, in the Caucasus mountain areas, in the timber felling area of Byelorussia, in the mines of the Ukraine and in the marshlands of Northwest Russia. More Chinese worked in the Far-Eastern region of Russia. In the gold mines of Amur, the Chinese labourers made up 80 per cent of the total work force. In the forests of Siberia and at the worksite of Haishenwei (Vladivostok) they underwent much difficult work. Their efforts to improve the economic life of the Far-Eastern area in Russia are immeasurable.

(9) CHANGES IN THE LIFE OF THE OVERSEAS CHINESE

In the last 20 to 30 years great changes have taken place in the life of the overseas Chinese, changes in their nationality and distribution, and in their political, economic and cultural life.

Eighty per cent of the overseas Chinese have become citizens of their countries of residence, thus becoming foreign citizens of Chinese origin. In a number of countries they now constitute a minority nationality, and in certain countries such as Singapore, the majority nationality. This is a great change in the history of the overseas Chinese.

The distribution of overseas Chinese has also changed to some extent. In recent years, besides those who have gone abroad from China's mainland, the number of compatriots from Hong Kong and Macao who have gone to Southeast Asia, the United States, Canada and Australia has grown daily. Quite a number of Taiwan compatriots have also gone to the United States, Canada, South America and other places. Of the persecuted refugees fleeing Viet Nam, a large number were overseas Chinese or Chinese descendants. Besides returning to China, or going to Thailand and Malaysia, they have gone to America, Europe and Australia.

Since the founding of New China, the social status of overseas Chinese has risen considerably. Most of them are proud of their strong socialist motherland, and many of them have devoted themselves to promoting friendship between China and their residing countries.

Of course, overseas Chinese have met with many difficulties and troubles. Because of the adverse current against China in some countries, especially recently in

Viet Nam, overseas Chinese and the local citizens of Chinese origin have encountered disasters. In some countries, parochial nationalists and racists have instituted laws of exclusion against Chinese. And Soviet hegemonists have added fuel to the flames. Consequently the just rights of the overseas Chinese have been infringed upon, even local citizens of Chinese origin have felt the threat. They have come to know that they must fight for themselves to win their equal rights.

Economic conditions of overseas Chinese have also changed greatly. At one time most of the overseas Chinese were said to live on three knives — kitchen knife, razor and scissors. This meant that they were engaged in businesses such as restaurants, barber shops and tailoring. In the United States, many overseas Chinese ran laundries or restaurants, while quite a number of overseas Chinese in Southeast Asia were workers or small traders. In the past 20 to 30 years, because of the development of the local economy and restrictions of commerce engaged in by overseas Chinese and local citizens of Chinese origin, many of them turned to running industrial enterprises or other modern undertakings. The number of joint enterprises run by the overseas Chinese and local industrialists have increased. In short, the economy of overseas Chinese and foreign citizens of Chinese origin has undergone distinctive changes, not only in terms of the types of trades, composition and scale of capital, but also in terms of the management and activity of their enterprises.

However, many difficulties still exist for overseas Chinese in the area of their economic development. Despite their contributions to the national economy of their residing countries, the governments in some regions have adopted policies fostering the "economy of the native inhabitants" and restricting the "economy of non-native inhabitants", thus hampering the natural economic development of overseas Chinese and local citizens of Chinese origin.

Overseas Chinese also have achieved distinct changes in education. In the past, most of them were labourers, poor people with little education when they emigrated. Now they and their descendants have received higher educations, and quite a number have become intellectuals. In recent decades the number of intellectual overseas Chinese or foreign citizens of Chinese origin has increased greatly, especially in the United States. It is estimated that of 120,000 to 130,000 first-class scientists and engineers in the United States, nearly 30,000 are overseas Chinese or foreign citizens of Chinese origin. Quite a number of these have become the mainstays of U.S. scientific research departments. For instance, the U.S. citizens of Chinese origin Chen-ning Yang. Tsung-dao Lee and Samuel C. C. Ting have won Nobel Prizes, and I. M. Pei and K. J. Lee have become world-famous architects. In the Federal Republic of Germany, Australia and Southeast Asia there are a considerable number of high-level overseas Chinese intellectuals who have made great contributions to the local development of science and technology.

2. CHINA'S POLICY CONCERNING OVERSEAS CHINESE

(1) THE BASIC PRINCIPLE AND SPECIFIC POLICIES

The overseas Chinese are a component part of the patriotic united front of the Chinese people, which has made and will continue to make outstanding contributions to China's revolution and construction. Therefore, the state attaches great importance to the affairs concerning overseas Chinese.

The basic principle and specific policies of the affairs concerning overseas Chinese have been worked out according to the tasks of the state at different periods and on the basis of the different conditions of overseas Chinese, returned overseas Chinese, and their families and relatives. At the founding of New China in 1949, the Chinese People's Political Consultative Conference adopted a Common Programme, which stipulated, in Article 58, that it was the government's intention ". . . to protect the proper rights and interests of Chinese residing abroad". The Constitution of the People's Republic of China, adopted in 1954, stipulated in Article 98 that it was the duty of the government ". . . to protect the proper rights and interests of Chinese residents abroad", while the new Constitution adopted in 1978 again confirmed that "the State protects the just rights and interests of overseas Chinese and their relatives" (Article 54). This shows the consistency of China's policies towards overseas Chinese affairs.

Overseas Chinese affairs can be divided into two areas, which are closely connected and complement each other.

Overseas Chinese affairs at home are handled according to the principle of giving equal treatment without any discrimination and giving appropriate preferential treatment to specifics so as to arouse the patriotic and socialist enthusiasm of the relatives of overseas Chinese and returned overseas Chinese and to lead them into active participation in China's socialist construction.

Overseas Chinese affairs abroad are handled according to the general policy of "unity, patriotism and friendship". The aim is to educate the overseas Chinese so that they will assist each other, protect their own just rights and interests, strengthen and consolidate patriotic unity, support the cause of construction and the unification of the motherland, and promote friendship with the local people. This policy also encourages overseas Chinese to change their nationality to that of their residing countries, to make contributions to economic development and cultural prosperity of their residing countries, to increase the relationship with the Chinese people at home and to promote the friendship between China and their residing countries.

(2) POLICIES TOWARDS OVERSEAS CHINESE AFFAIRS AT HOME

"Giving equal treatment without any discrimination and giving appropriate preferential treatment to specifics" is the basic principle adhered to in regard to overseas Chinese affairs at home. This principle reflects the reality and characteristics of the work in handling overseas Chinese affairs at home. On the one hand, as returned overseas Chinese and relatives of overseas Chinese are part of the Chinese people, they enjoy common rights and fulfil common obligations like other Chinese. On the other hand, they are different from other Chinese people. The members of their families are living separately in different societies, but have economic connections, keep close contact and often visit each other. Though overseas Chinese are Chinese citizens, they reside abroad in different circumstances. Therefore, "appropriate preferential treatment to specifics" is given them.

The two aspects of the principle of "giving equal treatment without any discrimination" and "giving appropriate preferential treatment to specifics" cannot be separated, but supplement each other. Only when the principle is carried out perfectly, can the two aspects be correctly handled; only when the relationship between overseas Chinese affairs and national affairs and the relationship between overseas Chinese affairs both at home and abroad are well handled, can the just rights and interests of the vast number of returned overseas Chinese and relatives of overseas Chinese be protected and can their patriotic enthusiasm both for their motherland and native towns be protected and encouraged.

As work concerning overseas Chinese affairs at home involves, to a large extent, foreign affairs, the correct handling of overseas Chinese affairs at home has much influence on China's relationship with other countries, and lays the foundation for the handling of overseas Chinese affairs abroad.

The main policies towards overseas Chinese affairs at home can be summed up as follows:

Correct Policy Towards the Relations Between Returned Overseas Chinese and Relatives of Overseas Chinese on the One Hand and Their Relatives and Friends Abroad on the Other. This policy refers to the relations between returned overseas Chinese and relatives of overseas Chinese on the one hand and their family members, relatives and friends abroad on the other, including financial relations, correspondence and visits to each other. These are normal relations. The government pays great attention to the correct handling of this question and criticizes erroneous viewpoints about it. The government clearly points out that the relations between returned overseas Chinese, relatives of overseas Chinese and their relatives and friends abroad are normal relations that should be encouraged and protected and given a positive role to play.

Accepting Overseas Chinese Students to Study in China. Overseas Chinese love their motherland and Chinese culture and hope that their sons and daughters will maintain traditional Chinese culture. Since the founding of New China, more and more overseas Chinese have sent their sons and daughters back to China to study. To meet the demands of overseas Chinese students who want to study in China, the People's Government formulated concrete policies and measures in accordance with the principles of "giving equal treatment without any discrimination and giving appropriate preferential treatment to specifics" and of "being free to come and go".

All overseas Chinese students, who have graduated from senior middle school or its equivalent, are entitled to enrole in Chinese institutions of higher learning, and may apply to return to China and enter their names for an entrance examination to study in any of the institutions of higher learning without any restriction.

The state has set up the Overseas Chinese University and Jinan University to enrol overseas Chinese students and students from Hong Kong, Macao and Taiwan. The Overseas Chinese University is a university of science and engineering located in Quanzhou, Fujian Province. Jinan University is a comprehensive university with faculties in arts, science, economics and medicine. For the convenience of overseas Chinese, Hong Kong, Macao and Taiwan students, the Overseas Chinese University and Jinan University have, since 1980, conducted entrance examinations earlier than those of the other universities. They also use different papers, and students are enrolled on a competitive basis.

Furthermore, Chinese language schools for overseas Chinese students have been set up in Beijing, Guangzhou and Jimei in Xiamen. In the latter two schools, special preparatory courses have been opened for overseas Chinese, Hong Kong, Macao and Taiwan students to take before the university entrance examination. The students are divided into different groups according to the subjects they choose, such as, literature and history, science and engineering, agriculture and medicine. After finishing the courses, they can take a university entrance examination. Those who fail in the examination can return to the schools for another year's study, if under the age limit. The three schools also have Chinese language departments and short-term Chinese language classes for overseas Chinese and foreign students of Chinese origin.

Like the other students, overseas Chinese students can apply for financial aid. During vacations they can return to their original residing places, and the price of their train and air tickets is set at the same price as it is for ordinary Chinese passengers.

Overseas Chinese students are given diplomas after they finish their studies and pass the examination. According to the principle of "being free to come and go", they may find jobs or continue their study in China, or go back to their original residing places.

Receiving Returned Overseas Chinese and Helping Them Settle Down. Since the founding of New China, many overseas Chinese, with patriotism and enthusiasm, have returned to China to help develop the country. Some of them were forced to leave their residing countries because of local discrimination against the Chinese or because of political persecution. Recently some specialists, scientists and engineers have come back to settle down and work in China.

The government's consistent policy towards returned overseas Chinese is: warm reception, appropriate arrangement and a proper settlement for each. The basic principles for the arrangements of returned overseas Chinese are as follows: finding them jobs in the countryside (mostly on state farms) according to their ancestral home places; for those having special skills, finding them jobs according to their ability; for the elderly who have relatives to look after them, making the arrangement so that they can live with their relatives. This policy was formulated in light of the principle of unified planning of proper arrangements and for the development of economy, with due consideration for the actual conditions and interests of the returned overseas Chinese. In its implementation, different localities make arrangements according to their local conditions and the request of the returned overseas Chinese.

The returned overseas Chinese love their motherland and support the Chinese Communist Party and socialism. The majority are working and studying hard at their posts, and doing their part for the country. Among them, a large number have became scientists, technicians, writers, artists and advanced workers, and some have been elected or promoted to leading posts. The state farms and factories for returned overseas Chinese have made great progress. The well-known Xinglong State Farm on Hainan Island, for instance, was only a piece of waste hilly land before Liberation. The first settlers on this piece of

land in 1951 were a group of 700 overseas Chinese refugees from Malaysia. Now it has become a large mul-
tiple-producing farm with over 20,000 people. The large
area of industrial crops it cultivates provides raw materials and products for the state. Another example is
the Overseas Chinese Plastics Factory in Fuzhou. When
it was founded 20 years ago there were only 20 overseas
Chinese refugees working there, but now it has become
a factory with 1,200 workers and staff. Its "White Dove"
brand plastic products are sold to more than 60 countries
and regions, earning foreign exchange for the state.

Policy Concerning Overseas Remittance. The state
protects overseas remittance and has adopted a policy of
"giving convenience to overseas remittance and serving
the overseas Chinese".

The State Council pointed out in its "Order for the
Implementation of the Policy of Protecting Overseas Remittance", issued on February 23, 1955: Overseas remittance is the earnings of overseas Chinese from their work
and is sent to support their families or relatives in China.
It is in the immediate interests of overseas Chinese and
is the life dependence of their families or relatives in China, and it is also their legitimate right to send or receive
overseas remittance. It benefits the country and the people. In the regions where the family members and relatives of overseas Chinese live in compact communities,
in particular, overseas remittance plays a positive role
in promoting the local economy and developing cultural
and public welfare undertakings. The Order also stipulates: Overseas remittance is the legitimate income of the
families and relatives of overseas Chinese; protecting
overseas remittance is not only the state's present policy
but is its long-term policy; no individuals or organiza-

tions are allowed to borrow by compulsion from the families and relatives of overseas Chinese; it is not allowed to withhold overseas remittance, inspect overseas remittance without permission or find an excuse to encroach on it in a disguised form; the families and relatives of overseas Chinese have the right to freedom in using their overseas remittance.

In relationship to overseas remittances, the state has adopted some necessary economic measures, one of which is the supply of materials for those receiving overseas remittances. Besides consumer goods, they are also supplied with construction materials for building houses.

It is general international practice that a country's overseas citizens remit money to support their families or relatives back home. The amount of money overseas Chinese remit back to China is very small compared with what overseas Chinese create locally. China appreciates the resonable policy adopted by many countries toward overseas Chinese remittances.

Overseas Chinese Investment and Donations. Because of their love for the motherland, their native towns and villages, overseas Chinese often make investments in China and help to develop the culture, education, public welfare and public service undertakings in their native places. This plays a positive role in speeding up the development of their native places and promotes the building of China's socialist economy.

In order to meet the wish of overseas Chinese who intend to help develop the motherland by making investments and in order to protect their interests, the state issued, in 1955, "Regulations Concerning the Use of State-Owned Waste Hills and Land by Overseas Chinese" and, in 1957, a policy for overseas Chinese investment encouraging them to invest in the State Overseas Chinese Investment Company. Overseas Chinese have developed, in recent years, new economic relations with China through cooperative management, joint ventures, compensation trade, and processing and assembling manufactured parts according to a supplied design. At the same time, the state encourages and organizes overseas Chinese, returned overseas Chinese and relatives of overseas Chinese to collect funds for establishing collective enterprises of various kinds. These collective enterprises not only promote the development of the local economy, but also provide more jobs and benefit returned overseas Chinese and the young relatives of overseas Chinese by training them in new skills.

The state welcomes and assists overseas Chinese in their desire to make donations that will help develop culture, education and public welfare. The state cites in appropriate forms those who make contributions to the development of the motherland and to their native homeland.

Protection of the Houses of Overseas Chinese. Though living in foreign countries, most overseas Chinese remember their ancestral homes and believe that a person residing elsewhere will finally return to his ancestral home. When finances permit, they remit money to China to build houses for their family members and relatives or for their own use when they become old and return to China to live for the rest of their lives.

The state stipulates clearly: "Protect the ownership of the houses of overseas Chinese, returned overseas Chinese and Chinese citizens who have foreign relatives. No organizations or individuals are allowed to occupy their houses on any pretext, and those which have already been occupied must be returned."

But, during the "cultural revolution" (1966-76), these government policies were put aside, and many houses of overseas Chinese were unlawfully occupied. In recent years, the people's government at all levels has paid more attention to this matter, and the regions and departments concerned have done a lot of work, with the result that most of the occupied houses have been returned. Those that have not, are only being occupied because of the lack of housing in China. Now the provinces, cities and departments concerned are adopting effective measures to solve this problem, taking this as an important issue in implementing overseas Chinese affairs.

Policy Concerning the Entering or Leaving of China by Overseas Chinese and Their Relatives. With proper reason, overseas Chinese, their relatives and returned overseas Chinese may apply to enter or leave China. This includes overseas Chinese coming back to China to trace their ancestral homes, visit relatives and friends, or as tourists. And it includes the relatives of overseas Chinese or returned overseas Chinese who apply to live abroad, visit relatives abroad, go abroad to accept property or a legacy, look after elderly parents abroad, or to reunite with their husbands, wives or children. These are their just rights, protected by the law.

The basic principle for the examination and approval of overseas Chinese and their relatives' entering and leaving China is flexible control that provides convenience and simplifies procedures. Those who apply to go to other countries and have that country's docu-

ments of entry and are in accord with the requirements
for leaving China usually get quick approval.

(3) POLICIES TOWARDS OVERSEAS
CHINESE AFFAIRS ABROAD

After the founding of New China, there were some
fundamental changes in the domestic and international
situation. Countries where overseas Chinese reside won
independence, one after another.   The question of
overseas Chinese became a matter concerning the relationship between China and the resident countries. The
anti-China forces and the Taiwan authorities carried out
many activities hostile to China among overseas Chinese.
They even incited some countries to persecute overseas
Chinese in an attempt to undermine the relationship
between China and these countries.   Because of this
situation, the Chinese government set itself the task of
protecting the fundamental interests of overseas Chinese
and improving the relations between China and the
countries where overseas Chinese reside.   The government decided to act according to the general principle
for China's foreign affairs; educate overseas Chinese to
follow China's foreign policy; not to take part in political
activities of the residing countries and to be voluntary
envoys of peace and friendship for the motherland so as
to promote friendly relations between China and the resident countries.   In the meantime, the principle of
"unity, patriotism and friendship" was formulated as a
guideline for directing the relations among overseas
Chinese, between overseas Chinese and their motherland,
and between overseas Chinese and their resident countries.

Principle of Unity, Patriotism and Friendship.
Overseas Chinese have a fine tradition of helping and
financially assisting each other, and of uniting for
existence. After the founding of New China, the
patriotism of overseas Chinese rose to a new height. In
some places, however, estrangement and dissensions still
exist among overseas Chinese due to geographical differences and political factions that affect the patriotic
unity of overseas Chinese. The state tries to educate all
overseas Chinese organizations, schools, presses and individuals to eliminate all dissensions and estrangement,
help each other, promote cooperation and form an extensive unity despite the difference in their native places,
occupations, class and religious beliefs.

Most of the overseas Chinese are working people.
They include workers, farmers, intellectuals, small
traders and handicraftsmen. A small part of them have
become bourgeoisie, mostly small or medium capitalists.
They have a tradition of loving their motherland and
their ancestral places and wish China to be prosperous
and strong. They have wide contacts with the local people and have made contributions to the economic and
cultural development of their residing countries. They
have also played a positive role in promoting the friendly
cooperation and economic relations between China and
their residing countries.

The patriotic united front of overseas Chinese is an
extensive united front, which can and should unite to
the fullest possible extent all those who can be united.
At present, the united front of overseas Chinese is constantly consolidating and expanding itself.

The patriotism of the Chinese people, including the
overseas Chinese people, is integrated with international-

ism. It is distinct from any conceited and selfish national chauvinism and from narrow nationalism. The state educates overseas Chinese to love their motherland and their residing countries, respect the local customs and habits, learn the local culture and languages, promote national cultural exchanges and develop friendly relations with China. It also educates overseas Chinese to develop the tradition of cooperation and militant friendship with the local people; take part in or help the local economic and cultural development, which are beneficial to the residing countries and the local people; support the local people in their struggles against colonialism, imperialism, hegemonism and for national independence; and promote the relations between China and their residing countries. This is in conformity not only with the immediate interests of the overseas Chinese, but also with the interests of their residing countries.

The Question of Dual Nationality of Overseas Chinese. Overseas Chinese mostly live in Southeast Asia. Since nationality in most of this region is determined by birthplace and the Chinese principle in the past was according to parentage, overseas Chinese and their descendants born locally usually have two nationalities — Chinese and the nationality of their residing countries. The question of dual nationality of overseas Chinese is a problem left over from history.

Because of this situation, the state decided to solve the problem of dual nationality with the Southeast Asian countries which had established diplomatic relations with China. In 1955, China signed a treaty on dual nationality with Indonesia, setting an example for the peaceful solution of international problems. The reasonable solution of this question was in conformity with the immediate interests of the overseas Chinese, helped develop the friendship between the two peoples and contributed to the maintenance of peace in Asia and in the world.

When receiving the former Chief Minister of Singapore, David Marshall, on October 9, 1956, the late Premier Zhou Enlai expressed his views on the nationality of Chinese in Singapore as follows:

1) The Chinese government is willing to see that the Singapore Chinese obtain their Singapore citizenship when they wish to do so and pledge their loyalty to the country in which they reside. The Chinese government believes that this will help promote their own interests, maintain the stability and peace of Singapore and develop a friendly relationship between China and Singapore.

2) Any Chinese living in Singapore, once they take out a Singapore citizenship, no longer will have their Chinese citizenship. Of course, their inherent national and cultural connections will still exist.

3) Any Chinese who has taken out a Singapore citizenship, at their own wishes, may get Chinese citizenship again if they legally give up their Singapore citizenship.

4) All overseas Chinese who maintain their Chinese citizenship must respect the laws and decrees of the government of their residing countries and not take part in local political activities, but their legitimate rights must be respected without any discrimination.

In his talk with the Burmese overseas Chinese in Rangoon on December 18, 1956, the late Premier Zhou Enlai also talked about the principles for solving the problem of dual nationality of overseas Chinese, and said that the obtaining of their residing country's citizenship by overseas Chinese at their own wishes meant "an addition to the population of Burma and also one more relative for China".

Later, the Chinese government solved the problem of dual nationality of those whose parents were Chinese and Mongolians after consultations with the People's Republic of Mongolia, in 1957, in the light of these principles. In a joint communique on the establishment of diplomatic relations between China and Malasia in May 1974, and in the joint communique of China and the Republic of the Philippines in June 1975, the Chinese government declared the principle that it does not recognize dual nationality.

The Nationality Law of the People's Republic of China, promulgated for implementation in 1981 by the Chinese government, was formulated in full consideration of the characteristics of China and the interests of overseas Chinese. The main feature of this nationality law is its declaration that China does not recognize the dual nationality of Chinese citizens. The law adopts a principle for determining nationality according to both parentage and birthplace. The method of determining nationality according to either parentage or birthplace alone is not used because of the bad results it may cause. This not only is in conformity with the tendency of international legislation concerning nationality laws, but also eliminates the source of dual nationality.

The Chinese government has always encouraged overseas Chinese to obtain the citizenship of their residing countries. After they have obtained the citizenship of their residing country, they automatically lose their Chinese citizenship and become citizens of their residing country. Therefore, they should pledge loyalty to the country they choose and take an active part in the development of that country. The Chinese government also welcomes those who want to keep their Chinese citizenship, but they are required to observe their residing country's laws, respect the local customs and habits and live in friendship with the local people. The Chinese government has the responsibility of protecting their legitimate rights and interests, and hopes the countries concerned will provide protection for them. The Chinese government hopes that overseas Chinese will play a role in promoting the friendship between the Chinese people and the people of their resident countries.

As for some countries which do not respect the wishes and interests of overseas Chinese, force them to change their nationality by unjust means, or even use violence to expel and persecute them, the Chinese government strongly opposes such actions because they violate the international law and human rights.

According to recent data, the greatest part of the more than 20 million people of Chinese origin in foreign countries have obtained their resident countries' citizenships. They have made great contributions to the development of the local economy and culture. At the same time, as relatives of the Chinese people, they sympathize and support China's construction and the cause of reunification of the motherland, and promote the friendly relations between their resident countries and China. This is understandable and also beneficial to the people of their residing countries and to the Chinese people.

Question About Chinese-Language Education of

Overseas Chinese. Many overseas Chinese who have lived for many generations abroad still use the Chinese language and maintain Chinese customs and habits. They have set up Chinese schools in their resident countries to educate their children in the Chinese language, national culture and traditions. After the founding of New China, more and more overseas Chinese have wanted to send their children back to China to study. Along with the rise of China's international status, overseas Chinese have shown greater enthusiasm in running Chinese schools and in studying the Chinese language.

To meet the needs of overseas Chinese wanting to send their children to study in China, the Chinese government has adopted various measures to assist overseas Chinese students in continuing their studies in China, while at the same time encouraging overseas Chinese to follow their tradition or running schools in their resident countries where their children can be educated. In overseas Chinese schools, the students not only study Chinese language, history and geography, but also the language, history and geography of the resident country. This provides better chances for the students to find jobs after finishing their study, serve overseas Chinese communities and the local people, and promote cultural exchanges and cooperation between China and their resident countries.

Overseas Chinese need to receive the culture and education of the residing countries and to learn the local languages. At the same time, overseas Chinese and those with Chinese origins usually wish to keep the traditions of their national language and a Chinese education. This is beneficial to the exchange of national cultures, the promotion of the friendship between China and their resident countries, and the development of local culture. In the spirit of the United Nations Charter, every nation has the freedom to keep its own national culture and language. This is a basic human right that must be respected. Some countries respect the just rights of overseas Chinese in keeping their Chinese education, which, the Chinese government and people think, is a principle of friendship and should be welcomed. Some other countries restrict or forbid the children of overseas Chinese and those with Chinese origin to receive an education in Chinese culture. This is against the United Nations Charter and a violation of human rights. The Chinese government and people are strongly against this practice.

Question About Overseas Chinese Organizations. There are many organizations among overseas Chinese that have been established in accordance with families, localities and trades, such as societies of the people with the same surname, associations of people from the same place, and unions of the same trade. Many of these organizations have a long history and a popular following, and exert a great influence among overseas Chinese. They are generally organizations that encourage mutual assistance among overseas Chinese; the collection of funds to establish schools, hospitals and other undertakings of public welfare; the finding of jobs for overseas Chinese; and the distribution of relief to widows, widowers and other poor overseas Chinese.

Since all the organizations were established according to families or localities, they have, since their beginning, close relations with the people who have the same ancestors and home towns in China. Relief and donations from overseas Chinese for the disaster areas and for building their home towns usually have been presented to China through these organizations. They have also played a positive role in the unity and patriotic activities of overseas Chinese and in safeguarding the just rights of overseas Chinese.

The existence of overseas Chinese organizations is beneficial to overseas Chinese and foreign citizens of Chinese origin in keeping their Chinese traditions, promoting relations between them and China, and in the development of friendship between the people of their resident countries and China.

The Role of Overseas Chinese in the Reunification of the Motherland. To promote the reunification of the mainland and Taiwan is a strong wish of the Chinese people of all nationalities, including compatriots in Taiwan and overseas Chinese.

When Ye Jianying, Chairman of the Standing Committee of the National People's Congress of the People's Republic of China, spoke to the Xinhua News Agency on September 30, 1981, making clear the policy and principles regarding the peaceful reunification of the mainland and Taiwan, he said, "We hope that our compatriots in Hong Kong and Macao and overseas Chinese will continue to make efforts to play a role as a bridge for the reunification of the motherland." This is a glorious and great historical mission for overseas Chinese.

There are at present a large number of overseas Chinese from Taiwan residing in foreign countries. Through contacts with overseas Chinese from the mainland, they have deepened their understanding of the motherland and want to see it with their own eyes. Many of them have come to China to look for their ancestral places, visit relatives, make a tour or settle down. The number is increasing daily. This has played a positive role in establishing contacts between the mainland and Taiwan, developing communication between the people on both sides of the Taiwan Strait and deepening their mutual understanding. Surely, overseas Chinese will play an even more important role in the reunification of the motherland in the future.

3. INSTITUTIONS OF OVERSEAS CHINESE AFFAIRS AND ORGANIZATIONS OF RETURNED OVERSEAS CHINESE

(1) STATE INSTITUTIONS OF OVERSEAS CHINESE AFFAIRS

The Overseas Chinese Affairs Commission of the People's Republic of China. Founded in 1949, this was the administration in charge of China's overseas Chinese affairs until 1970. Offices were set up in places where large numbers of returned overseas Chinese and relatives of overseas Chinese lived.

After its founding, the Overseas Chinese Affairs Commission implemented the principles and policies of the state concerning overseas Chinese affairs and achieved great progress. It aroused the patriotism and socialist enthusiasm of returned overseas Chinese and the relatives of overseas Chinese, and encouraged overseas Chinese's love for their motherland and their support for the development of China's socialist economy.

The Overseas Chinese Affairs Commission was dissolved in 1970 in accordance with the conditions at that time.

The Overseas Chinese Affairs Office of the State Council. Founded in 1978, this is now the administration in charge of China's overseas Chinese affairs.

The office's main tasks are: to study and formulate the principles and policies governing the work of overseas Chinese affairs both at home and abroad; to examine and supervise the implementation of policies governing the work of overseas Chinese affairs by localities and departments concerned; to protect and arouse the enthusiasm of overseas Chinese for their motherland and home towns; to encourage and guide returned overseas Chinese and the relatives of overseas Chinese and unite with overseas Chinese in contributing to the development of China's socialist material and spiritual civilization, the early reunification of the mainland and Taiwan and the safeguarding of world peace.

Organizations in charge of overseas Chinese affairs have also been set up in places where large numbers of returned overseas Chinese and the relatives of overseas Chinese live.

(2) ORGANIZATION OF RETURNED OVERSEAS CHINESE

The All-China Association of Returned Overseas Chinese, founded in 1956, is a people's organization uniting returned overseas Chinese from all walks of life throughout the country. Corresponding local organizations have been set up in places where large numbers of returned overseas Chinese and the relatives of overseas Chinese live.

The association's task is to encourage and guide returned overseas Chinese and the relatives of overseas

Chinese and unite with overseas Chinese in foreign countries to contribute to the development of China's socialist
material and spiritual civilization and to the early reunification of the mainland and Taiwan. Article 50 of the
Constitution of China stipulates that "The People's Republic of China protects the legitimate rights and interests of Chinese nationals residing abroad and protects
the lawful rights and interests of returned overseas
Chinese and of the family members of Chinese nationals
residing abroad." The association protects the legitimate
rights and interests of returned overseas Chinese and of
the family members of overseas Chinese and helps
departments concerned to popularize and implement the
state policies governing overseas Chinese affairs.

The First National Congress of Returned Overseas
Chinese was held in October 1956, in Beijing, when the
All-China Association of Returned Overseas Chinese
was founded.   Its Second National Congress was held,
also in Beijing, in December 1978.

(3) INSTITUTIONS OF HIGHER LEARNING FOR OVERSEAS CHINESE

Jinan University. Jinan University is located in
Guangzhou, Guangdong Province, and has a long history.
Its predecessor was the Jinan School, founded in Nanjing
in 1907, which mainly enrolled children of overseas Chinese.

Jinan University has now become a comprehensive
university mainly enrolling overseas Chinese students,
students from Hong Kong, Macao and Taiwan, children
of returned overseas Chinese, and relatives of overseas
Chinese. The university has a medical college, a college

of economics, and departments of mathematics, physics, chemistry, biology, Chinese, foreign languages, history, and journalism. The College of Economics provides a shorter course of accounting and the Chinese department has a special course in the Chinese language. To enroll more students, the university has, since 1980, set up four sub-departments and two junior college courses for non-resident students who pay the tuition fee themselves. In addition, the university has a full-time secondary school of physics and chemistry and a nursing class. It had 2,300 students (including graduate students) in the first half of 1981.

Jinan University has a dozen research institutes, including the Institute of Southeast Asian Studies, Overseas Chinese Institute, Institute of Economics, Orthopaedic Surgery Research Office, Office for the Application of Computers in Medicine, and Research Office of Immunology. These employ 260 researchers and are now undertaking 85 projects of scientific and medical research. Reproduction immunity, genetic engineering and biomedical engineering are some of the major research projects of the state that are being conducted by the Jinan institutes. There are also 83 projects of social science and art.

The university has nearly 100 laboratories. Its library has more than 800,000 books and over 3,300 periodicals. Some of these books and teaching facilities were donated by overseas Chinese and compatriots in Hong Kong and Macao.

Jinan University has a board of directors composed of a few dozen well-known personages at home and abroad.

Overseas Chinese University. The Overseas Chinese University, founded in 1960, is a comprehensive university in Quanzhou, Fujian Province. It closed in 1970 and reopened in 1978.

In the 10 years from 1960 to 1970, the university accepted overseas Chinese students from 17 foreign countries and regions and students from Hong Kong and Macao, totalling 2,300, and trained many of them into specialists. After it reopened in 1978, the university was changed into a school of science and engineering, with the latter as the main subject. It has six departments: mathematics, physics, chemistry, civil engineering, mechanical engineering and chemical engineering. And it now has 800 students.

The Overseas Chinese University has a board of directors composed of well-known personages at home and abroad.

Overseas Correspondence College of Xiamen University. Originally a department of Xiamen University, founded in 1956, the correspondence college, since its founding, has accepted 10,000 correspondence students from more than 30 countries and regions.

The Overseas Correspondence College provides lessons in the Chinese language, traditional Chinese medicine and acupuncture. It gives opportunities to study for overseas Chinese, foreign students in other countries and compatriots in Hong Kong and Macao, and helps to promote cultural exchanges and friendly relations between China and foreign countries.

(4) STATE OVERSEAS CHINESE FARMS

From the early years after the founding of New China through the 1960s, the state set up 41 overseas Chinese farms and three factories in Guangdong, Fujian, Guangxi and Yunnan as workplaces for nearly 100,000 returned overseas Chinese and overseas Chinese refugees. After 1978, 44 more overseas Chinese farms and forestry centres and eight overseas Chinese factories were set up. Nearly 200,000 workers were recruited to work in them. Thus the total number of overseas Chinese farms and forestry centres reached 85 and factories 11. They are distributed in Guangdong, Guangxi, Fujian, Yunnan, Jiangxi and Jilin.

Overseas Chinese farms, forestry centres and factories are places where overseas Chinese can make a living and receive an education. They are under the dual leadership of the Overseas Chinese Affairs Office of the State Council and the corresponding office in the province or autonomous region, with the latter providing the main leadership.

Overseas Chinese farms and forestry centres are mostly situated in the sub-tropical zone in southern China. Many of the returned overseas Chinese and overseas Chinese refugees are from Southeast Asia, and some of them have experience in cultivating tropical and sub-tropical industrial crops. Therefore, the farms and forestry centres have specialized in the production of rubber, oil palm, pepper, sisal hemp, fruits, sugar-cane and other industrial crops. For many years, the overseas Chinese farms and forestry centres have developed industrial crops in a planned way, according to local conditions, and have built their own industries and processing factories. Many farms, forestry centres and factories make products for export. The Xinglong State Overseas Chinese Farm is the most successful one among them.

The Xinglong Farm, founded in 1952, is located in

Wanning County on Hainan Island. By 1981, the farm
had accepted 18,000 returned overseas Chinese and overseas Chinese refugees from 20 foreign countries and regions. In the past 30 years, the farm has built a tropical
plantation of 7,666 hectares, in which rubber plants account for 3,333 hectares.   In 1981, the farm produced
2,100 tons of dry rubber. They have also increased their
production of pepper and coffee. In addition, the farm
attaches importance to the production of rice and peanuts.
It runs a dozen small factories such as a farm machinery
repair shop, grain and oil processing factory, agricultural
and sideline products processing factory, rubber processing factory, brick kiln and hydro-power station.

(5) CHINA TRAVEL SERVICE AND OVERSEAS CHINESE TRAVEL SERVICE

The China Travel Service and Overseas Chinese Travel Service make arrangements for overseas Chinese, Chinese compatriots from Taiwan, Hong Kong and Macao
and foreigners of Chinese origin to travel in China and
visit their relatives.   Its head office is in Beijing, and it
has branches in all provinces, municipalities and autonomous regions and in all major cities opened to tourists,
famous tourist spots, and cities and county towns in
Guangdong and Fujian which are the native places of
overseas Chinese.

Chapter Four

RELIGION

1. AN OUTLINE OF RELIGION IN NEW CHINA

⌐The major religions in China are Buddhism, Taoism, Islam, and Christianity, which includes Catholicism and Protestantism. Among these, Buddhism and Taoism have the longest history and have exercised the greatest influence on the culture of China, historically as well as contemporaneously.⌐ Christianity was introduced into China mainly after the Opium War of 1840, and most Chinese Christians live in the coastal provinces. Islam, though introduced earlier than Christianity, has had a wide influence only among the Huis, Uygurs, Kazaks and seven other ethnic minorities. Contacts have long existed between Chinese Buddhists, Muslims and Christians and their co-religionists in other countries.

⌐After the founding of the People's Republic of China, the government adopted the policy of granting freedom for religious beliefs. The Constitution of the People's Republic of China ensures this freedom for religious beliefs, giving every citizen the right to believe in any religion they might choose or not to believe in any religion. Religious and non-religious people enjoy equal rights socially and politically, and both are protected by the law. Religions, big or small, are equal politically, and there is no one religion that dominates the others.⌐

The government does not interfere with believers' religious activities, and it protects their temples and churches in carrying out religious activities. To ensure mutual respect between believers and non-believers and normal social order, the government requires that religious activities be limited to the premises of temples, mosques and churches, and that non-believers abstain from going into temples, mosques and churches to propagate atheism. The government maintains a policy of uniting and educating the patriotic religious leaders of the different religions and of respecting their religious beliefs without discrimination. Delegates to the People's Congresses and Political Consultative Conferences at all levels include religious personages.

The government has, under the jurisdiction of the State Council, a special bureau and departments at all levels that are in charge of religious affairs. Buddhism, Taoism, Islam and Christianity also have their own national and local organizations to handle their affairs independently. They publish their own journals, and maintain their own religious institutes of higher learning, such as the Islamic Theological Institute, the Nanking Union Theological Seminary and the Institute of Chinese Buddhism. These institutes train new clergy and researchers.

Many religious bodies and personages have exchanged visits with their counterparts in other countries, thus increasing mutual understanding and friendship. The establishment and functioning of these religious organizations have helped to implement the government's policy on freedom of religious belief, strengthen the unity of nationalities, develop the socialist economy and safeguard world peace.

To promote academic research in the field of religion,

the Chinese Academy of Social Sciences has established the Institute of World Religions with special departments of Buddhism, Islamism, Christianity, the Chinese history of atheism and the foreign history of atheism.

The freedom for religious beliefs suffered a severe setback during the "cultural revolution". Religious organizations were then abolished. Many temples, mosques and churches were either closed or destroyed, and religious activities came to a halt.

After 1976, when the "cultural revolution" ended, the temples, mosques and churches were renovated or reopened, and their activities were resumed.

2. BUDDHISM

The Buddhist religion was founded by Prince Siddhartha, son of King Suddhodana (Pure Rice King) of Kapilavastu in central India (present-day Nepal), between the 6th and 5th centuries B.C. Prince Siddhartha was also known as Sakyamuni, which means "the wise man of the Sakya clan". Generally the Buddhist doctrines encompass three points: The world is impermanent and eventually will be destroyed; all the things and beings are unreal; and the aim of a person's life is to achieve eternal tranquility.

(1) BUDDHISM IN CHINA

The Spread of Buddhism. Buddhism was introduced into the regions inhabited by the Han people, the largest ethnic group in China, around the 1st century. According to written records, during the reign of Emperor Aidi of the Western Han Dynasty, in 2 B.C., an envoy named Yin Cun from Indoscythe went to Chang'an (today's Xi'an) to impart Buddhist sutras verbally to a Chinese scholar named Jing Lu. Emperor Mingdi (A.D. 57-75) of the Eastern Han Dynasty later sent a mission to the Western Regions to search for Buddhist scriptures. He also built China's first Buddhist temple, known as the White Horse Temple, in Luoyang. During the Wei and Jin dynasties (A.D. 220-420) the influence of Buddhism spread widely.

The Buddhist doctrines eventually became integrated with traditional Chinese ethics and religious concepts. Xuan Xue (metaphysics) was very popular among the ruling classes at that time. The Buddhist doctrine of Prajna (believing that the whole universe is unreal) had many things in common with Xuan Xue, and the two soon became one. During the Southern and Northern Dynasties (A.D. 420-589) the ruling class further helped the spread of Buddhism by building temples and monasteries, translating Buddhist sutras, and constructing grottoes. Many famous monks, scholars and teachers emerged at this time. By the Sui and Tang dynasties (581-907), Buddhism had reached its apex of popularity and splendour, and different sects of Buddhism had been formed in China. Among these were the Tiantai Sect, the Three Satra Sect, the Huayan (Avatamsaka) Sect, the Chan (Dhyana) Sect, the Pure Land Sect, the Esoteric Sect, the Faxiang (Dharmalaksana) Sect and the Vinaya Sect. All these sects were later introduced into Korea, Japan and Viet Nam.

Over a long period, Buddhism gradually took roots in the feudal society of China, intermingling with Confucian and Taoist thought to become an important part of the intellectual history of China. It had a strong popular appeal, and its ideas made a notable impact on Chinese philosophy, morality, literature and art.

Buddhism has a wide influence among China's national minorities. The followers of a Buddhist sect called Lamaism live mostly in areas inhabited by Tibetans, Mongolians, Tus, Qiangs and Yugurs. In the 7th century, King Songzan Gambo of Tubo (Tibet), influenced by his two wives, Princess Wen Cheng of the Tang emperor's household and Princess Bhrkuti of Nepal, converted to Buddhism. By the 8th century Indian monks had come to Tibet to spread Esoterism, a sect of Buddhism. Esoterism, the Buddhism of the Hans, which had also been introduced to Tibet, and the original religion of Tibet intermingled and developed into Lamaism.

Lama means "upper-class person" or "teacher" in Tibetan. After the 10th century, Lamaism itself had formed several different sects, the Red Sect (Nyingmapa), the Flower Sect (Sakyapa), the White Sect (Kagyurpa) and the Yellow Sect (Gelugpa). The Yellow Sect was founded fairly late in 14th century by Tsongkhapa, who wanted to effect reforms in Lamaism. Lamas of the Yellow Sect are not allowed to marry. Later Tsongkhapa's two principal diciples, the First Dalai and the First Bainqen, were assigned to be leaders of the sect. In 1546, in the time of the Third Dalai, the system of choosing the Dalai's successor by discovering his "reincarnation" was established, and in 1653, in the time of the Fifth Dalai, the same system of choosing Bainqen's successor was established. In the 15th and 16th centuries, the Yellow Sect grew into the dominant sect of Lamaism and spread from Tibet to Sichuan, Qinghai, Gansu and Mongolia.

Hinayana, or Lesser Vehicle Buddhism, was introduced to south China from Burma in the 13th century, and its believers today are mainly people from the Dai, Blang, Benglong and Va ethnic minorities in Yunnan Province.

Famous Monks. The long history of Chinese Buddhism produced many famous monks, such as Fa Xian, Xuan Zang and Jian Zhen.

Fa Xian of the Eastern Jin Dynasty, surnamed Gong before he became a monk, was a pioneer traveller, who went to India to study and translate scriptures. In A.D. 399, at the age of 65, Fa Xian, together with some other monks, went west from Chang'an to seek Buddhist scriptures. His journey lasted 14 years and covered more than 30 countries, including northern, western, central and eastern India and Sri Lanka. He brought back many Buddhist scriptures to China and translated them from Sanskrit into Chinese. In his book, *A Record of the Buddhist Countries*, he related what he had observed during his journey. The book provides valuable reference material for those studying the history, geography and communications of ancient India and the Western Regions.

Xuan Zang of the Tang Dynasty, originally named Chen Wei, was a Buddhist scholar, traveller and translator who, along with Kumarajiva and Paramartha, was one of the greatest translators in the history of Chinese Buddhism. In A.D. 627, he set out from Chang'an for India. He passed through Gansu, Xinjiang and Central Asia and, after much hardship, finally reached India, where he lived for 15 years visiting many famous temples. He studied Buddhist classics and learned the Buddhist doctrines from Indian monk scholars. After returning to Chang'an, he translated 75 Buddhist scriptures

(1,335 volumes) into Chinese. He also wrote an account of his trip, entitled *Records of Western Travels,* an important reference to researchers in the study of the history and geography of ancient India, Nepal, and Pakistan, as well as Central Asia. The novel *Journey to the West,* is a mythological account of his trip to India.

Jian Zhen of the Tang Dynasty, originally surnamed Chunyu, tried five times to sail from Yangzhou in Jiangsu Province to Japan, at the invitation of Japanese Buddhists. On his sixth try, accompanied by 24 disciples, he finally reached southern Kyushu. The year was A.D. 754, and he was then 67. The next year, in Nara, Japan's capital at that time, he began to preach and spread the Buddhist teachings. He was the founder of the Ritsugaku Sect in Japan. Accompanying him to Japan were architects, artists, doctors and pharmacists. They took a large library and many works of art with them, and did much to stimulate the cultural flow between the two countries. The magnificent Tang-style Toshodai Temple at Nara still looks much the same as it did when it was built under Jian Zhen's direction. Jian Zhen lived for nearly 10 years in Japan and died there in 763.

Buddhist Temples. The earliest Buddhist temple built in China was the White Horse Temple in Luoyang, Henan Province. According to tradition, in A.D. 67, during the reign of Emperor Mingdi of the Eastern Han Dynasty, two Indian monks, Gobharana and Kashyapa Matanga, brought Buddhist sutras on a white horse to Luoyang from the Western Regions. They helped to build this temple.

Prior to the 3rd century, most monks followed the old disciplines of Buddhism that forbade monks to keep property and required them to live by begging alms. But after the 3rd century, financed by imperial families and nobles who gave rewards and donations, temples, pagodas and grottoes were built across China. By the Western Jin Dynasty (265-316), 180 temples had been built in Chang'an and Luoyang alone. Those built by the Eastern Jin Dynasty (317-420) numbered 10 times as many. Many of these temples possessed a large amount of land and were in fact, feudal manors.

A Chinese Buddhist temple generally consists of a Hall of the Heavenly Kings, a Sanctuary of the Buddha, a Hall of Guanyin (Goddess of Mercy), and a repository for the Tripitaka, or scriptures.

The Sanctuary of the Buddha, the main hall in a Buddhist temple, often houses an image of Sakyamuni. In many temples, it houses the trinity of the three ages: Kasyapa, the Buddha of the Past; Sakyamuni, the Buddha of the Present; and Maitreya ("Laughing Buddha"), the Buddha of the Future. Another trinity often found in Chinese temples is formed with Bhaisajyaguru (the Buddha of Medicine), representing the East; Sakyamuni, representing the native place; and Amitabha, representing the West. Along the two walls of the main hall are generally a group of arhats, or images of Buddhist notables. The number of arhats is usually 16, but is sometimes 18 in the temples erected in the Han areas.

The repository mainly houses the Tripitaka, which consists of three parts. The first is a collection of Sakyamuni's teachings; the second, the Buddhist rules and regulations; and the third, explanations of Buddhist doctrines. According to the *Kaiyuan Records of Sakyamuni's Teachings* of the Tang Dynasty, the Buddhist scriptures translated into Chinese by scholars of successive dynasties and the Chinese Buddhist writings after the religion spread to China already numbered 1,076 titles in 5,048 volumes by the time of the Kaiyuan Reign (739-740). More titles were later added to this collection.

Monasteries of the different sects in Chinese Buddhism house images of different Buddhas, and the arrangement of sanctuaries varies from sect to sect. For instance, every monastery of the Yellow Sect of Lamaism houses an image of Tsongkhapa, and every temple of the Dhyana Sect must have a Meditation Hall.

Temple Organizations, Buddhist Rules and Regulations, and Festivals. The temples of different sects vary somewhat in their organization. But, in general, each temple has an abbot, a resident priest (or a superintendent) and various monks responsible for receiving pilgrims and conducting religious activities. The personnel in some temples was very large before Liberation.

The Buddhist rules and regulations from India underwent some changes after they were imported into China. For instance, in India, monks were required only to have their heads shaved, to beg for alms and to be clothed in Kasaya robes. Chinese monks followed these rules in the early years. But after the Buddhist rules were translated into the Han language in the mid-3rd century, Chinese monks became fully ordained Bikkhu monks. In the 4th century Bikkuni nuns appeared for the first time. In the Buddhist rules established by the Venerable Dao An during the Eastern Jin Dynasty, all Chinese monks and nuns were required to have the surname Shi (the Chinese abbreviation for Sakyamuni) instead of their fathers' surnames. In the 6th century, Emperor Wudi of the Liang Dynasty prohibited monks and nuns from consuming anything that originated from an animal. By the Tang Dynasty (618-907), Monk Huai Hai of the Dhyana

Sect formulated *Huai Hai's Rules,* a complete set of rules for Dhyana temples. There are different rules for different kinds of believers. Secular believers are called lay Buddhists. New monks and nuns who have not yet been initiated are called novices, and there are fewer rules imposed on them. Altogether there are 250 rules for initiated monks to follow and 348 for initiated nuns.

The major Chinese Buddhist festivals are:

1)   Birthday of Buddha: The birthday of Sakyamuni is on the eighth day of the fourth lunar month in areas inhabited by the Han ethnic group, on the 15th day of the fourth lunar month in areas where Mongolian and Tibetan national minorities live, and on any of the 10 days around the Qingming ("Clear Brightness") Festival in areas where the Dai national minority lives. According to Buddhist traditions, Sakyamuni was bathed in a fragrant rain that spurted from the month of a dragon. Therefore, on the birthday of Sakyamuni, Buddhists bathe his image with fragrant water. This is called "Bathing the Buddha".

2)   The date of Buddha's attainment of Nirvana: This usually falls on the 15th day of the second lunar month. But the year of Buddha's death was recorded differently by different groups of early Buddhists and so the Buddhist Age (the first year fell on the year of Buddha's death) is calculated differently in different parts of China.

3)   The date of Buddha's attainment of Buddhahood: This day marks Sakyamuni's attainment of Buddhahood underneath a bo tree. It usually falls on the eighth day of the 12th lunar month.

4)   Guanyin festivals: There are three Guanyin festivals in China, namely her birth on the 19th day of the

second lunar month, her attainment of nunhood on the
19th day of the sixth lunar month, and her attainment of
enlightenment on the 19th day of the ninth lunar month.

(2) BUDDHISM AFTER LIBERATION

Before Liberation, many Buddhist believers also
worshipped the gods and their ancestors. Thus Buddhist
believers in China were usually also Taoists. There were
about 500,000 monks and nuns and 40,000 monasteries
and temples in China before Liberation, though it is hard
to tell the exact number of Buddhist believers in China.

In the early years after Liberation, many eminent
Buddhists demanded reforms in Buddhism and the aboli-
tion of the feudal system of oppression in Buddhist
monasteries and temples. Monks and nuns began to take
part in agriculture, forestry or handicraft production
when they were not engaged in religious activities, thus
earning their own living.

Freedom of Buddhist beliefs has been guaranteed by
the Constitution since Liberation, and Buddhist religious
activities have been protected by the government. Buddhists enjoy equal political rights with the other people of
the country, and representatives of Buddhist circles are
elected as deputies to the people's congresses and as members of the Chinese People's Political Consultative Conference at various levels. Here they discuss state affairs
with people from other circles. A fairly large number of
Buddhists have made significant contributions to industrial and agricultural production and to the cultural, medical and other social welfares of China.

Buddhist Organizations In 1953 the First Buddhist

Conference was held. It was sponsored by distinguished
Buddhist leaders, such as Chen Mingshu, Ye Gongchuo,
Yuan Ying, Neng Hai, Xu Yun, Shirob Jaltso, Gelazang,
Liuxia, Tudengtaba, Danbarijie, Duojizhandong, Lü
Cheng, Zhao Puchu, Zhou Shujia and Guo Peng. The Chinese Buddhist Association, a national organization, was
founded at that conference. It held its second, third and
fourth conferences in 1957, 1962 and 1980 respectively. It
has done a great deal to unite Buddhists for the development of the socialist economy; help the government in carrying out the policy of freedom for religious beliefs; train
Buddhist students; do research on the history and theology of Buddhism; protect and evaluate Buddhist relics,
and repair and maintain famous monasteries. The Chinese Buddhist Association was chaired by Yuan Ying and
the Venerable Shirob Jaltso for the first and second terms.
Bainqen Erdini Qoigyi Gyaincain and Ying Ci were its
honorary chairmen and the Venerable Shirob Jaltso, its
chairman, for the third term. Its fourth, or present, honorary chairman is Bainqen Erdini, while Zhao Puchu
serves as its chairman.

In 1956 the Institute of Chinese Buddhism was established as the highest institution of Buddhist learning
in China. It has an undergraduate course, special subject
training course and a research department. The Institute
had graduated 380 students by 1966. Most of these graduates returned to their homes to work for local Buddhist associations and to maintain famous monasteries.
Some remained at the Institute to continue their studies.
They have made great progress in the study of Buddhism
and have translated, edited and written many essays
about the history and theory of Buddhism. The Institute
was closed during the "cultural revolution". It reopened

in 1980. It is located in the Fayuan Temple, one of the oldest temples in Beijing. A branch college of the Institute was founded recently on Mount Lingyan, near Suzhou in Jiangsu Province.

The journal *Fa Yin (Buddhist Voice),* sponsored by the Chinese Buddhist Association, began publication in February 1981. It prints academic papers on Buddhism and translations of articles written by authors from China's different ethnic groups as well as foreign scholars. The Chinese Buddhist Association also has its own library and museum. A Buddhist scripture printing house has been set up by the modern Buddhist scholar Yang Renshan. It is located in Nanjing, Jiangsu Province.

The Protection and Maintenance of Monasteries. To implement its policy of freedom for religious beliefs, the Chinese government maintains and protects leading monasteries in China. For example, the stupa of the Lingguang Temple on the Western Hills near Beijing, which was destroyed by the eight Allied Armies in 1900, was rebuilt by the government in 1960. Its opening ceremony was held in 1964. A "tooth of the Buddha" (Sakyamuni's tooth) is preserved in the stupa. According to tradition, there are still two preserved teeth of Buddha. One is in Sri Lanka and the other is in this stupa near Beijing. Another example is the Yunju Temple of Beijing, where more than 10,000 tablets were unearthed after Liberation. On these tablets are Buddhist scriptures engraved over a period of more than 1,000 years, from the Sui to the Ming dynasties. These tablets have been classified, and rubbings have been made of them.

Great numbers of murals and carvings depicting Buddhist religious methology have been found in the world-famous Mogao Grottoes of Dunhuang, Longmen

Grottoes of Luoyang and Yungang Grottoes of Datong. They have been put under state protection. The state also protects and grants special funds for the maintenance of other famous Buddhist temples and lamaseries, such as the Ci'en Temple in Xi'an, Fayuan Temple and Yonghegong Lamasery in Beijing, Lingyin Temple in Hangzhou, White Horse Temple in Luoyang, Shaolin Temple in Dengfeng County of Henan Province, the Jokhan, Sera and Drepung lamaseries in Tibet, the Kumbum Lamasery in Qinghai Province and the Labrang Lamasery in Gansu Province. On religious festival days, grand ceremonies are held in these monasteries with the attendance of many Buddhists.

International Exchange. Since 1949, Chinese Buddhists have established contacts with Buddhist organizations and individual Buddhists in more than 20 countries and regions. Friendly visits have been exchanged between them. In 1955 and 1961 respectively, at the request of the governments of Burma and Ceylon (now Sri Lanka), the Chinese Buddhist Association took the Buddha's tooth to these countries for their Buddhists to adore. In 1962, Chinese and Japanese Buddhists, historians and artists jointly organized commemorative activities marking the 1200th anniversary of the death of Jian Zhen in Japan. In 1964, on the 1300th anniversary of the death of Xuan Zang, the Chinese Buddhist Association hosted Buddhist delegations from Japan, Sri Lanka, Kampuchea, Viet Nam and six other countries. The anniversary was commemorated by the completion of the rebuilt stupa in Beijing to house the Buddha's tooth relic.

The Chinese Buddhist Association has sent delegations to Kampuchea and India for international Buddhist conferences and for the commemoration of the 2500th

anniversary of the Nirvana of Sakyamuni Buddha. In the
spring of 1980, the image of Jian Zhen was flown from
Japan to China. Chinese Buddhists welcomed it and put
it on display in Yangzhou, Jian Zhen's hometown, and in
Beijing. All this has promoted mutual understanding
and friendship between the Chinese people and the peoples of other countries, and between the Buddhists of
China and those of the rest of the world.

3. TAOISM

(1) HISTORY OF TAOISM

Taoism is indigenous to China. Taking form as a religion during the reign of Emperor Shundi (A.D. 125-144)
of the Eastern Han Dynasty, it has a history of more than
1,800 years. In feudal China, Taoism together with Buddhism exerted great influence over the country's economy,
culture and political thinking, and it was one of the spiritual mainstays of the feudal ruling class.

It was during the reign of Emperor Shundi that
Zhang Ling founded the Heavenly Teacher Sect, also
known as the Five Piculs of Rice Sect, in the Heming
Mountains in Sichuan Province. Zhang Ling became the
sect's Heavenly Teacher, and they made Lao Zi their supreme god, taking Lao Zi's *Tao De Jing* as their canon.
Thus, with the mystical interpretation of the philosophical
views of Lao Zi at its core, the Taoist doctrine was built
on ancient witchcraft and recipes for immortality.

Towards the end of the Eastern Han Dynasty, a peasant rebel leader named Zhang Jiao established another

Opening ceremony of the Mount Lingyan College (Suzhou, Jiangsu Province) of the Chinese Institute of Buddhism.

Longmen Grottoes in Luoyang, Henan Province —
one of the three famous Buddhist grottoes in China.

Consecration ceremony in honour of Bishop Fu Tieshan held by the Xuanwumen Catholic Church in Beijing.

The Nanjing Union Theological Seminary in Jiangsu Province.

Guangta Pagoda in the ancient Guangta Pagoda
Mosque in Guangzhou, Guangdong Province.

Professor Li Songshen (*left*) in the Civil Engineering
Department of the Overseas Chinese University in
Quanzhou instructing a student from overseas.

Imam An Shi-wei reciting the scripture in the Dongsi Mosque in Beijing.

A corner of the dairy of the Guanghua Overseas
Chinese Livestock Farm in Guangdong Province.

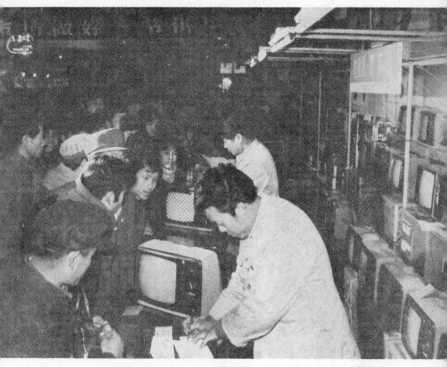

Inhabitants in Tianjin picking out and buying TV sets.

A watermelon stand on
he street in Beijing.

Inside a new peasant home on the outskirts of Wuxi, Jiangsu Province.

Gulangyu Park, a favourite place for retired workers in Xiamen.

Taoist sect called Tai Ping Tao. Propagating the doctrines of this sect in north China, he managed to convert
several hundred thousand peasants. The uprising he led
in A.D. 184 dealt a heavy blow to the feudal empire.
When the sect was banned, following the repression of
the revolt, its members went underground and operated
secretly among the people.

Meanwhile, Zhang Ling's descendants carried on in
Sichuan Province and at Hanzhong in Shaanxi Province.
The government that Zhang Lu, Zhang Ling's grandson,
established in Hanzhong existed for 27 years (188-215).
His efforts to spread the gospel of the Five Piculs of Rice
Sect resulted in the conversion of large sections of the
population. By the Western and Eastern Jin dynasties,
the Five Piculs of Rice Sect had become a major religious
movement in the country. Towards the end of the
Eastern Jin Dynasty, a peasant uprising organized by
Sun En and Lu Xun in the name of this sect went un-
defeated for more than a decade.

During the Southern and Northern Dynasties, the
feudal rulers, in an attempt to prevent further peasant
uprisings, reformed early Taoism so that it might help
them in their efforts to control the peasants. In the
north, Kou Qianzhi, a Taoist priest at Mount Songshan,
took the Confucian concept of "assisting the government
and helping the people" to create a New Heavenly
Teacher Sect, or Northern Heavenly Teacher Sect, a
faith that advocated increased religious ritual and meditation. In the south, Lu Xiujing, a priest at Mount Lu-
shan, revised the Taoist scriptures and formulated a new
set of sacrificial rites to incorporate those already followed by the Han people. His sect was known as the Southern
Heavenly Teacher Sect.

Taoism gained in popularity during the Tang and Song dynasties (960-1279) as a result of the support given it by the feudal ruling class. Its monasteries and temples grew in grandeur and were to be found all over the country. And, like Buddhist temples, they were granted special privileges. Big Taoist temples became not only places of worship but also the owners of large tracts of land. During the Yuan Dynasty (1271-1368), the Northern and Southern sects and other Taoist sects merged to form a new sect called the True Unity Sect.

In 1167, during the Kin Dynasty, Wang Chongyang founded the Complete Unity Sect in Shandong Province. In the succeeding Yuan Dynasty, the high opinion the Yuan emperor held of Qiu Chuji, Wang's disciple, gave this sect momentary popularity. From then on the True Unity Sect and the Complete Unity Sect were the two major sects of Taoism.

The True Unity Sect preached the beliefs of "driving out devils by calling in the gods" and "averting disasters by prayer". Its priests were allowed to marry and did not have to abstain from meat and wine, except during the special diet periods.

The Complete Unity Sect emphasized self-cultivation and immortality. Its priests were required to renounce home life, practise vegetarianism and stay unmarried. Its religious discipline included the Commandments of the Gods, of Middle Supremacy and of Primary Truth.

Taoism declined during the Qing Dynasty (1644-1911) but, as it had become a popular religious faith, it continued to exert some influence over a section of the population. By 1949, there were about 40,000 Taoist priests and nuns, and 20,000 monasteries and temples.

(2) PHILOSOPHICAL TAOISM

The word "Tao" means "the Way" and is the basic concept in Taoism.   According to the *Tao De Jing*, all things in the universe are created by Tao, which exists beyond the physical sense of men; Tao produces things spontaneously without will or goal. It moves in endless cycles and never changes. But nothing that is produced by Tao lasts forever. Taoism makes a mysterious and religious interpretation of Tao, regarding Tao as God, the creator of the world and of all beings.

Taoism has a god for almost everything —the sun, moon, stars, wind, rain, thunder, lightning, mountains, rivers and the country. The religion also has gods of the Town, Land, Kitchen, Door and Wealth. At the head of these gods are the Supreme Patriarch (Lao Zi) and the Jade Emperor. These gods are enshrined in Taoist monasteries and temples. In old China, their icons were also to be found in many homes. People worshipped the God of Wealth, called Marshal Zhao, in the hope of achieving a big fortune. The God of the Door was supposed to keep away demons, and the God of the Kitchen was believed to be "in charge of every household's fortune and misfortune". It was said that every year he would report to the Jade Emperor on the good and evil of the household he supervized. He was worshipped on the 23rd day of the 12th month of the lunar year, the day he reportedly ascended to Heaven, and again on Spring Festival Eve when he reportedly returned.

Taoists believe in immortality. The immortals, so they say, breathe in wind, drink dew, ride the clouds and wander about. They are detached and free from all earthly worries. Men and women can expect to "achieve

the Way" and longevity, even immortality, if they give
themselves up to unremmitting cultivation. The fairy
tale "The Eight Immortals Crossing the Sea", long
popular among the people, has its origin in Taoism.

Taoism has a great many classics. *The Collection of
Taoist Classics,* prepared in the Ming Dynasty, consists
of as many as 5,485 volumes. The number in use as
prayer books, however, is not great. They are mainly
the *Tao De Jing,* a philosophical poem of over 5,000
characters in rhyme; the *Canon of Quietism,* which
teaches people to keep clear of earthly desires so as to
achieve peace of soul and mind; *Canon of the Jade
Emperor,* which extols the Jade Emperor and begs the
immortals for happiness and blessings; and the *Yellow
Yard Classics,* written in verse with seven characters
to a line, which teaches the ways of Taoist cultivation.

(3) TAOISM IN NEW CHINA

Changes in the Life of Taoist Priests. Before Liberation, the priests of the True Unity Sect lived on contributions and donations from worshippers and on memorial
ceremonies for the dead that they were hired to execute.
The priests of the Complete Unity Sect lived in the
woods, depending on monastery property, temple fairs,
and donations for an income. A small number of roaming priests supported themselves by selling medicinal
herbs and telling fortunes. Since Liberation, most
priests have settled down to productive occupations.
Those who live in cities are often factory workers or
handicraftsmen; those in the countryside engage in farming or forestry; and those at scenic spots and historical
sites are employed in tourism. Religious activities, in-

cluding dieting and memorial ceremonies, take place inside the monasteries and temples. Rituals involving self-cultivation are performed whenever and wherever the priests find time.

The Taoist Association. After Liberation, the different Taoist sects gradually merged into one, thus ending the division between the Complete Unity Sect and True Unity Sect. In April 1957, following the First Congress of Taoists in Beijing, the Chinese Taoist Association was founded. This association assists the government in implementing its policy of freedom for religious beliefs; contacts and unites Taoist believers throughout the country with the aim of preserving and promoting the fine traditions of Taoism; sees to it that its members, under the leadership of the people's government, work in national interest; supports the country's socialist construction, and joins in the defence of world peace. The Taoist Congress elects a council of directors who, in turn, choose the members of its standing committee, chairman, deputy chairmen and secretary-general. The first chairman of the Council of the Chinese Taoist Association was Yue Chongdai. The chairman succeeding him was Chen Yingning, and then Li Yuhang. The association has its office in the White Cloud Monastery in Beijing.

The Taoists have a publication of their own, *The Journal of the Taoist Association*. There is also a training centre for future Taoists. On the basis of the historical documents and records of Taoism they have collected and studied, the Research Section of the Taoist Association has put out two books, *An Anthology of Taoist Historical Documents* and *An Outline History of Chinese Taoism*. This section runs a permanent exhibition of selected Taoist cultural relics from their collection at the White Cloud Monastery. In recent years, the Chinese Taoist Association has received many visiting scholars of Taoism from abroad. The interchange of information from such visits has contributed to the growth of friendship.

The Protection and Renovation of Taoist Monasteries and Temples. There are many famous Taoist monasteries. Those of the Complete Unity Sect include the White Cloud Monastery in Beijing, Black Sheep Monastery in Chengdu, Supreme Purity Monastery in Shenyang, and Tower Terrace at Zhouzhi in Shaanxi Province. Those of the True Unity Sect include the Upper Purity Monastery at Longhu Mountain in Guixi County, Jiangxi Province; the Yuanfu Monastery at Maoshan Mountain in Jurong County, Jiangsu Province; and the Upper True Monastery at Qionglong Mountain in Suzhou. These monasteries, most of which are magnificent palace-like buildings, have in recent years been repaired or renovated with government funds and have been put under state protection.

4. ISLAM

(1) ISLAM IN CHINA

The Spread of Islam. Exactly when Islam reached China remains a matter of controversy, but the generally accepted date is around A.D. 651, when Emperor Gaozong of the Tang Dynasty was on the throne. For two dynasties after that, the Tang and Song, the land and sea routes to China provided contacts with the Arab world and its Islam religion. The land route, used by merchants, diplomats and military men, went through Persia and Afghanistan before it terminated in China's Northwest. The sea route began in the Arabian Sea, and passed through the Bay of Bengal and the Straits of Malacca before it reached China's Guangzhou, Quanzhou, Hangzhou and Yangzhou ports. Those who travelled by this route were mostly Arab and Persian merchants, many of whom later settled in China and married Chinese women. Their descendants were Chinese Muslims.

During the western military expeditions of Genghis Khan in the early 13th century, a large number of Muslims recruited from Central and West Asia came to China. Among these Muslim soldiers there were artisans and petty government officials, referred to as "Hui" in the *History of the Yuan Dynasty*, who fought for Kublai Khan in the war that unified China. These Hui soldiers brought Islam to wherever they were garrisoned as farmer-soldiers.

During the Yuan Dynasty, the court extended special privileges to the Muslims for their "contributions to the founding of the dynasty". Schools for Huis were opened, mosques were built all over the country and Muslims became government officials of various ranks. Sai Dianchi of the Yuan Dynasty, for example, was at different times governor of Shaanxi, Sichuan and Yunnan provinces. By decree of the emperors of early Ming and Qing dynasties, Islam also enjoyed state protection. This made it possible for Islam to thrive in China.

Most Chinese Muslims are Hanafiyahites of the Sunni Sect. But after it was brought to China, Islam also spawned many new sects such as "Qadim", meaning following the ancient tradition, and "Ikhwan", meaning brotherhood.

During the late Ming and early Qing dynasties,
Chinese scholars of Islamism grew in number. Centred
in Nanjing and Suzhou, they busily engaged themselves
in translating Islamic teachings and introducing Arabic
culture into China. Among the important Islamic works
that they translated were *The Truth of Islam, Comprehensive Book of Islamic Sciences, The Right Way of
Islam,* and *The Book of Islamic Rules.*

Islamism has a large following among 10 of China's
minority nationalities. These are the Hui, Uygur,
Kazak, Tatar, Kirgiz, Tajik, Ozbek, Dongxiang, Salar
and Bonan peoples. The number of believers totals
about 10 million in China. They live mostly in north-
western China, except for the Huis who are scattered
all over the country.

Famous Mosques. Most of the mosques in China
are constructed in palace style. In Xinjiang and other
places, there are mosques built in the traditional Islamic
style — a structure with a dome, or a tapering tower
from which Islamic leaders can call the people to prayer.
Every mosque contains a hall of worship in which there
is a *minbar* (pulpit) where the imam delivers sermons;
a place for washing the face, hands and feet before each
service; south and north halls where the imam teaches
Islamic classics, and a tower of *bang* from which the
call to prayer is issued.

China has many mosques noted either for their magnificence and spacious yards or for their long history.
For instance, the Guangta Pagoda Mosque in Guangzhou
and the Qingjing Mosque in Quanzhou were built by
Persian and Arab merchants during the Tang and Song
dynasties. The Guangta Pagoda Mosque, also called the
Huaisheng Mosque, was built some 1,300 years ago and

is one of the earliest mosques in China's coastal areas. With a flight of stairs spiralling round a central pillar, the 36-metre-high pagoda inside the mosque is unique in style. Now with renewed magnificence and grandeur after renovation, the ancient mosque and its pagoda are open to Muslims and tourists from abroad. The Qing-jing Mosque in Quanzhou, modelled after the mosques of Damascus, was built in 1009, during the Northern Song Dynasty. Magnificent and grand, the mosque is strongly Arabic in its architectural design.   ,

The Niujie Mosque in Beijing is one of the five largest mosques in China. Built in 996, during the North-ern Song Dynasty, and covering an area of 6,000 square metres, the mosque has gone through four enlargements in reaching its present shape. With upturned eaves and painted rafters and brackets, the main hall is construct-ed in the style of a Chinese palace. But its interior is typically Arabic in design. The hall, 600 square metres in size, holds more than 1,000 worshippers. Buried un-der the mosque are two imams who came to China as missionaries. These were Ahmad Butani, who died in 1280; and Imadi-Ldin, who died in 1283. The tombstones erected at the time of their death are inscribed in Arabic. Each day the mosque receives nearly 100 worshippers, and, during the Lesser Bairam and Corban Bairam, as many as 1,000.

Other mosques built during the Tang and Song dynasties include the Pheonix Mosque in Hangzhou, the Libai Mosque in Yangzhou and the Huajue Mosque in Xi'an. Mosques constructed in the later Yuan and Ming dynasties include the Dongsi Mosque in Beijing and the Aitgar Mosque at Kashi in Xinjiang. During the Qing Dynasty other mosques were erected in Kunming, Tian-

jin, Shenyang, Shanghai and Chengdu. Most of these
went through expansion or reconstruction before they
assumed their present sizes.

These mosques not only testify to the spread of
Islam in China, but they throw light on some aspects
of the life-style of minority peoples. They are also fine
examples for the study of Chinese architecture during
the period of their erection. Since Liberation, these
mosques have been renovated several times and are listed as cultural relics under government protection.

Islamic Festivals. Three major Islamic festivals
are observed in China. The first is Lesser Bairam, held
on the first day of the 10th month of the Muslim
calendar immediately after the month of fasting called
Ramandan ends. The second is Corban Bairam, or the
day of sacrifice, which falls on the 10th day of the 12th
month on the Islamic calendar. This day has its origins
in ancient Arabic mythology. The Prophet Abraham, so
the story goes, was told by Allah on this day to kill his
son Ismail, but when Abrabam was about to execute the
order, Allah told him to kill a sheep instead. Thus every
year on Corban Bairam, the Arabs offer a sacrifice of
sheep. The third is Mohammed's birthday, which falls
on the 12th day of the third month on the Islamic
calendar. Mohammed was also believed to have died
on this day, and so it is also his death anniversary.

Lesser Bairam, or the day of breaking the fast, is
a highly festive day among China's Muslims. During
the previous month of fasting, no one is allowed to eat
between dawn and sunset. When the month comes to
an end, the Muslims celebrate the breaking of the fast
by eating sumptuous meals.

Corban Bairam is celebrated in Beijing, Xinjiang,

Gansu, Ningxia and some other places. In northwest China, Muslims celebrate this day by feasting guests on beef and mutton, and by exchanging gifts. In the Kazak areas, the Han people are invited by native herdsmen to their yurts, where they are treated to mutton, fried pastry and milk tea.

(2) ISLAM IN POST-LIBERATION CHINA

Muslims enjoy religious freedom in New China as do the advocates of other religious faiths. In early 1952 the Chinese Islamic leaders Burhan, Depusheng, Makien and Pang Shiqian began to organize a Chinese Islamic association. In May of the following year, the First Islamic Conference was held in Beijing, and the Chinese Islamic Association, a national organization of Chinese Muslims, was formed. Burhan was its chairman for the first three consecutive terms. When Burhan left office to become honorary chairman, the chairmanship went to Zhang Jie. The association has local branches throughout the country.

In April 1955, the association established the Islamic Theological Institute in Beijing. This has since trained many Islamic missionaries and scholars. The association has also sponsored research activities on Islamic history and theology in recent years, and the Koran and other Islamic classics that it publishes have had many impressions. *Muslim in China,* the association's magazine, which was first published in 1957, resumed publication in early 1982.

The areas inhabited by China's 10 minority peoples of the Islam faith have regional autonomy. These areas

are the Xinjiang Uygur Autonomous Region, Ningxia
Hui Autonomous Region, four autonomous prefectures
and 13 autonomous counties. The Muslims there are
represented in the people's congresses, Political Consultative Conferences and people's governments at all levels.

The customs of the Muslims are respected in China.
Their special needs in terms of food, funerals and the
observance of religious festivals are protected by the
people's government.

Since 1955, the Chinese Islamic Association has
organized 11 pilgrimages to Mecca. Some of the pilgrims,
on their return journey, paid friendly visits to Islamic
countries in Asia and Africa. For many years, Islamic
scholars and noted Muslim leaders from many countries
have visited China at the invitation of the association,
and the members of the association have visited many
Islamic countries as guests of the Muslims there. Delegations sent by the association have attended many international conferences, such as the Asian and African
Islamic Conference held in Bandung in 1964, the Islamic
Ideology Symposium held in Algeria in 1979 and 1980,
and the Islamic Symposium held in Tokyo in 1981. Such
international contacts have contributed to the understanding and friendship between the Chinese people
and the people of various Muslim countries.

5.   CATHOLICISM

(1)   CATHOLICISM IN CHINA

In A.D. 635, when Emperor Taizong of the Tang
Dynasty was on the throne, members of a Catholic sect

known as Nestorians arrived in Shaanxi Province in China. They established a church that flourished for 210 years and then sank into oblivion. In A.D. 1245, Italian and French missionaries arrived in China. The religion that came with them was called Yeliwen by the Chinese. Like its predeccessor, Yeliwen also died out after a period of time. In the 16th century, at the time of colonialist plunder, the Portuguese came to the East. Macao, which they seized from China in 1557, soon became a base for Western missionaries.

In 1582, Matteo Ricci, an Italian Jesuit, came to China. He arrived in Beijing in 1601. Among the presents he brought for Emperor Shenzong of the Ming Dynasty were some chime clocks. He soon became a friend of Xu Guangqi, Minister of Rites to the Ming court. Ricci propagated the doctrines of Catholicism and introduced Western astronomy, calendar-making and mathematics. With the permission of Emperor Shenzong, he built a Catholic church in Beijing. From then on, China saw an inflow of missionaries of various Catholic orders and congregations.

Towards the end of the Ming Dynasty, there were an estimated 40,000 Catholics in China. During the Qing Dynasty, according to a 1700 survey, the number of the Catholics increased to nearly 300,000. Faced with the growing influence of this foreign church, the Qing court decided to take measures to outlaw Catholicism. In 1705, out of resentment against the Pope and missionaries who forbade Chinese Catholics to worship Confucius and their own ancestors, Emperor Kangxi banned the Roman Catholic Church. As a result, the number of the Catholics dropped sharply. By the end of the 18th century, there were only 200,000 Catholics in China.

The Western capitalist powers, following the Opium
War of 1840, forced open the gate of China and imposed
a series of unequal treaties on the Qing government. In
1844, the government had to lift the ban on Catholicism.
Two years later, it returned confiscated properties to the
church. Thus, the Roman Catholic Church recovered its
legitimate status in China.

The Treaties of Tientsin (Tianjin), concluded at the
end of the Second Opium War in 1857, stipulated that
foreign missionaries operating in inland China were
entitled to the protection of local governments. The
Convention of Peking (Beijing) of 1860 went even
further, providing missionaries with the right to rent
land and put up buildings in the provinces of China.
This gave foreign missionaries the freedom to take their
religion into the interior of China and set up churches
there. As these missionaries sometimes forcibly seized
land from the Chinese, interfered with the administration of justice and bullied both government and people,
they became the targets of public outbursts of anger
throughout China. Between 1859 and 1900 there were
as many as 60 such "church cases".

After the 1911 Revolution, Catholicism in China
grew stronger because the feudal warlords and the Kuomintang government inherited the policy of national
betrayal of the Qing government. The 1946 "National
Statistics on Catholicism in China" showed that by that
year there were about 3,270,000 Catholics.

The Catholic Church in old China was colonial and
semi-colonial in its status. Before 1946, the Chinese
Catholic church operated on a "mission area system"
under the jurisdiction of the Holy See's Congregation for
the Propogation of the Faith, the organization in charge

of church affairs in colonial countries. In 1946, the Vatican put the Chinese Catholic church on "the hierarchical system" by which there were 20 apostolic provinces and 143 dioceses, but the church remained under the same jurisdiction, and the Chinese Catholics clearly were left with no power. For the 20 apostolic provinces, there were only 5 Chinese archbishops, and of all the bishops in the 143 dioceses, only 20 were Chinese. This was obviously unfair, but, under the circumstances, nothing could be done to change the situation, although it was censured, even attacked, by some Chinese ecclesiastics and their congregations.

(2) THE CHINESE PATRIOTIC CATHOLIC ASSOCIATION

The founding of the People's Republic of China in October 1949 not only marked a turning-point in Chinese history but it also ushered in a new era for Chinese Catholics. In November 1951, a "Declaration of Independence and Reform of the Catholic Church", signed by Father Wang Liangzuo in Sichuan Province and some 500 other Catholics, set in motion a patriotic movement against imperialism. A vast number of Chinese Catholics joined in this movement. In July 1956, the Office of the Preparatory Committee of the Chinese Patriotic Catholic Association was set up in Beijing. At the National Congress of Catholics, held in Beijing from July 15 to August 2 in 1957, the Chinese Patriotic Catholic Association was founded. The congress adopted its constitution, and elected Pi Shushi, Archbishop of the Shenyang diocese, as chairman of the association.

An organization of patriotic and devoted Catholics,

the association vows to work for the unity of priests and bishops across the country, promote patriotism, take an active part in the country's socialist construction and patriotic movements, defend world peace, and assist the government in carrying out its policy of freedom for religious beliefs. In order to frustrate the Vatican in its attempt to interfere in China's internal affairs and to turn the Chinese Catholic Church into a tool against New China, the Congress decided to put an end to the colonial and semi-colonial status that the Chinese Catholic Church was subjected to in old China, and adopted a policy of independence and self-administration. The Second Congress of the association was held in 1962. It brought the work of the association to a high stage and re-elected Pi Shushi chairman of the association.

In May 1980, the Chinese Patriotic Catholic Association held its third congress in Beijing. A total of 198 bishops, priests and laymen from 26 provinces, municipalities and autonomous regions attended. The congress reviewed the work of the association in the previous 18 years, decided on its future tasks and elected Bishop Zong Huaide chairman of the association.

(3) ADMINISTRATION OF THE CHINESE CATHOLIC CHURCH

Between 1958 and 1962, the 50-odd dioceses in China elected their own bishops and consecrated them, thus turning the Chinese Catholic Church, which had long been under foreign manipulation, into an independent church administered by Chinese Catholics themselves. In May 1980, the National Congress of Chinese Catholics was held in Beijing. This produced two national organizations — the Chinese Catholic Affairs Committee and the Chinese College of Bishops.

According to Item Two of the committee's regulations, the committee, "in accordance with the teachings of the Holy Bible, carries on the traditional spirit of mission that originated with Jesus Christ and His apostles; preaches the Gospel; promotes the cause of glorification of God and the salvation of souls; sees to it that the ecclesiastics and their congregations observe the Commandments of God; remains faithful to the principles of independence and democratic self-administration; makes decisions on important church affairs and administers the Chinese Catholic Church efficiently". The National Congress of Chinese Catholics is the supreme body for the administration of church affairs. During its recess, the Chinese Catholic Affairs Committee is in charge of the implementation of its decisions. Bishop Zhang Jiashu has been elected chairman of the committee.

The Chinese College of Bishops, headed by Bishop Zhang Jiashu, is "composed of the bishops of the various dioceses. Its tasks are to study and interpret the Catholic creed and canon, exchange experience in missionary work and promote friendly ties with Catholics abroad" (Item Seven of the committee's regulations).

The clergy and laymen throughout the country, with their patriotism deepened through study, took an active part in socialist construction. Many of them were chosen as model or advanced workers. True to the spirit of independence and self-administration, the church carried on its normal religious activities. But during the "cultural revolution", as happened for all other religious bodies in China, the Catholic Church suffered a great deal and its religious activities were discontinued. In 1977, the government's policy of freedom for religious beliefs was reaffirmed. The churches have since been re-opened, and church activities have been resumed.

(4) CHINESE CATHOLIC CHURCHES AND RELIGIOUS ACTIVITIES

There are many well-known Catholic churches in the various dioceses of China. Among them are the Ruose Church and Xuanwumen Catholic Church in Beijing, the Xujiahui Catholic Church in Shanghai, the Stone House Church in Guangzhou and the Catholic Church at Shanghai Street in Hankou.

The Xuanwumen Catholic Church in Beijing, built in 1650 under the supervision of the German priest Adam Schall, is now the residence of the bishop of the Beijing diocese. The church, built in Gothic style, consists of living quarters for the priests, an observatory, a library, an instruments room and a hall large enough for 1,000 people to attend Mass at one time. The hall is complete with an alter, tabernacle, holy lamp, priests' changeroom, and confessional. The choir is at the back of the church. The Stone House Church in Guangzhou, built over 100 years ago, has also been renovated and reopened.

Every Sunday, Chinese Catholics go to Mass in the various churches. The churches also perform wedding ceremonies, give Requiem masses and baptize new converts. In 1980, for instance, about 100 converts were baptized in the Catholic churches of Beijing. The ordination of new priests, discontinued for more than 10 years, has been resumed. On Easter and Christmas,

Catholics come to the churches to attend High or Low Mass.

In recent years, the Chinese Catholic Church in various parts of the country and the Chinese Patriotic Catholic Association have been hosts to overseas Chinese, compatriots from Taiwan, Hong Kong and Macao, Catholic clergy and lay people, government officials, and experts from abroad. These contacts have helped the participants understand each other better. The Chinese Patriotic Association and its chapters have sorted out the historical materials of the Catholic Church that they have collected. Among the various journals they publish, *Chinese Catholicism* is a national publication edited jointly by the Chinese Patriotic Catholic Association and the Chinese Catholic Affairs Committee. In 1980, the committee decided to set up a Chinese Catholic Seminary to train Catholic clergy and theologians.

6. PROTESTANTISM

(1) PROTESTANTISM IN CHINA

Protestantism reached China in the 19th century. In 1807, during the Qing Dynasty, Robert Morrison, a pastor of the London Mission became the first Protestant missionary to reach China. This was a time when China was still a backward feudal country living in self-imposed isolation, a victim of European colonialist powers bent on external expansion and aggression. Acting through the East India Company, Britain dumped large quantities of opium on China. The British opium ships also brought the first groups of Western missionaries to China.   In order to plunder China's wealth, Western colonialist countries crashed open China's door with their gun-boats and imposed a series of unequal treaties on the country.   These treaties, drafted with the help of some of the missionaries, protected the missionaries in propagating Protestantism in China. Thus Protestantism, from its first entry into China, was identified with the aggression of Western colonialist powers.

Morrison's arrival in China was followed by an influx of missionaries from Britain, France, the U.S., Germany and other countries. Protected by the unequal treaties and in total disregard of Chinese laws, they extended the influence of their church far into China's interior. In the 90 years between 1842, when the Treaty of Nanking (Nanjing) was concluded, and 1932, as many as 154 Protestant sects were established in China. Each of these sects was sub-divided into those controlled separately by Britain, the U.S., France and Germany. In their efforts to expand the influence of their churches, the representatives of these sects worked hand in glove with each other and at the same time plotted against or even conflicted openly with each other. Thus a pattern of spheres of influence was established: Shanghai and Xiamen were mainly Anglican, Ningbo was Baptist, Sichuan Province was Methodist and North China was Presbyterian. According to statistics taken shortly before Liberation, the number of Chinese Protestants was more than 700,000.

After the Yi He Tuan Movement (the Boxer Uprising) of 1900, the Protestant missionaries and their foreign missions moved into the field of culture. They opened schools, set up hospitals and other cultural and

religious institutions in China. On the surface these
foreign missions seemed to have brought modern technology and civilization to China, but their ultimate aim
was to assist colonialist expansion in the country and to
secure colonialist gains. They were therefore resented
and hated by patriotic Chinese Christians and the Chinese people in general. Patriotic Chinese Protestants
also resented the dominance of foreign missions in the
management of personnel and economic affairs of the
church because this reduced the Chinese Protestant
Church to a position of dependence on them. In the
early 20th century, a few farsighted Chinese Christian
leaders with a deep sense of national dignity tried to
"create a Church of our own" by promoting love for
their country and their religion among Chinese
Christians. Their objective of getting rid of the control
of Western missionaries, however, was not obtainable
within the historical context of that time.

(2) THE THREE-SELF PATRIOTIC MOVEMENT

The founding of New China prepared the ground
for an independent and self-governing Chinese Protestant church. In the summer of 1950, 40 prominent
Chinese Christians headed by the Rev. Wu Yaozong
signed a declaration on "Efforts to Be Made by Chinese
Christians for the Building of a New China". The declaration spoke against the control of the foreign missions
over the Chinese church and called on both clergy and
laity of Chinese Protestant Christianity to govern their
own church, support it with their own economic contributions and do their own evangelestic work. These

principles later became known as the "Three Selfs" (self-administration, self-support and self-propagation). The declaration received enthusiastic response from Chinese Christians. They signed the document, and soon the Three-Self Patriotic Movement developed vigorously throughout the country.

In July 1954, a National Conference of Chinese Christians was held in Beijing. This conference announced the establishment of the Three-Self Patriotic Movement Committee to be based in Shanghai, and elected Wu Yaozong as the committee's chairman. The movement strengthened the ties between Christians and non-Christians in China because they shared political and national commitments. The Three-Self Movement also united the various Chinese churches, thus eliminating the sectarian prejudices brought to China by Western missionaries.

(3) CHINESE CHRISTIAN COUNCIL AND ITS ACTIVITIES

In October 1980, the Third National Conference of Chinese Christians was held in Nanjing. In addition to the formation of the Third Three-Self Patriotic Movement Committee with Ding Guangxun (K. H. Ting) as its chairman, this conference established the Chinese Christian Council, an organization in charge of promoting church work, with Ding Guangxun as its president. Today, the Protestant churches in various parts of China, brought together through this council, have become one entity, free of sectarianism. This has been possible because the Chinese Protestant church was too young to have formed any deep-seated sectarian prejudices and because Christians share a common faith.

Since 1977, following the "cultural revolution", church activities have been resumed. The Bible has been reprinted to meet the religious needs of Protestants, and, in 1981, the Nanjing Union Theological Seminary was reopened. In addition, the Three-Self Patriotic Movement Committee and the Chinese Christian Council have resumed the publication of their journal, *Tian Feng* (*The Gospel*). They have also published a number of religious books. In the past few years, Chinese Protestants and Christians in other countries have visited each other. These contacts, based on equality and mutual respect, have increased the understanding between Chinese and foreign Christians and have contributed to the cause of world peace.

Chapter Five

EMPLOYMENT, WAGES AND WELFARE

1. EMPLOYMENT

(1) A BASIC OUTLINE

With the development of the national economy since the founding of the People's Republic, the number of people employed in China's urban areas has increased 12.9 times. In 1949, there were some 8.09 million workers and staff and 7.24 million self-employed working people throughout the country; by the end of 1980, the number of workers and staff reached 104.44 million. Among them, 80.19 million were working in the enterprises under ownership by the whole people and 24.25 million were working in enterprises under collective ownership.

The educational and technical level of workers and staff has also been raised as the state trains specialized personnel at colleges or technical secondary schools who on graduation are assigned to work by the state, local governments or ministries concerned. From 1949 to 1980 there were 3.17 million college graduates (an increase of 17 times over the 185,000 graduated from college in the 20 years before 1947.) From 1931 to 1946, there were only 547,000 secondary specialized school graduates and 1.43 million secondary technical graduates. From

Number of Workers and Staff in Departments Under Ownership by the Whole People (In 10,000 persons)

Department \ Year	1952	1957	1965	1975	1980
Industry	510	748	1,238	2,691	3,246
Building Industry	104.8	271.4	383	558.5	674.4
Agriculture, Forestry, Water Conservancy, Meteorology	23.9	112.3	422	723.3	805.2
Transportation, Post and Telecommunications	112.9	166.5	245	399.5	479.3
Commerce, Food and Drink, Service Trades	292.3	488.7	550	829.5	1,082.1
Science, Culture and Education, Public Health	239.2	327.3	533	755.1	1,071.1
City Public Utilities	4.1	21.8	44	74.7	121.8
Finance	34.4	36.2	36	36.6	62.5
Government and Mass Organizations	258.5	278.9	287	357.6	477.1
Total	1,580	2,451	3,738	6,426	8,019

Number of Workers and Staff in Departments
Under Collective Ownership in Urban Areas
(In 10,000 persons)

Year Department	1965	1977	1978	1979	1980
Industry	505.4	1,142	1,215	1,327.7	1,428.3
Building Industry	93.5	157	174.5	219.1	236.5
Agriculture, Forestry, Animal Husbandry Fishery, Sideline Production	72.3	51.4	59.2	51.6	48.1
Transportation	172.6	188.9	204.3	218.6	215.8
Commerce, Food and Drink, Service Trades	200.3	203.1	211.3	259.4	302.1
Culture and Education, Public Health	117.8	123	128.4	132.9	130.5
Administrative Departments	6.3	14	14.2	17	13.7
Other Departments	58.4	37	41.1	47.2	49.8
Total	1,226.6	1,916.4	2,048	2,273.5	2,424.8

1949 to 1980, 5.8 million graduated from secondary specialized schools.

Enjoying the equal right to work, women in China have become an important component of the country's labour force. Starting in 1949 with an estimated 600,000 women workers in enterprises under ownership by the whole people, the number of women workers had by 1980 grown to 24.73 million or 30.8 per cent of the general work force. In some areas, the percentage of women workers was higher: in textile, tailoring and the leather industry, women accounted for 33.9 per cent of workers; in culture and education, public health, social welfare and scientific research, they accounted for 37.4 per cent. Women peasants account for 50 per cent of people engaged in farm labour. Women are also taking on increasing influence as experts, model workers, advanced workers and leaders.

(2) EMPLOYMENT PROBLEMS OVER THE PAST 30 YEARS

Just after Liberation, the government began to tackle in several ways the problem of four million unemployed. It provided jobs for those working in the enterprises of bureaucrat capitalism as well as for the army and government personnel of the Kuomingtang. It gave aid to private businesses to prevent bankruptcy and the dismissal of workers and staff. In addition to recruiting workers and staff according to production needs, the government also gave temperary jobs and encouraged the unemployed to organize themselves for productive work instead of waiting for government relief. Training was provided for those who needed new skills to find employment. As a result of these arrangements, production quickly recovered and developed. By 1958, more than four million previously unemployed people had jobs.

From 1953 to 1957, some 950,000 young people in cities and towns who had reached the work age got jobs. During this period, the system of unified recruiting and deploying manpower was established. State labour departments were responsible for providing personnel for state or private business recruitment and to coordinate with the responsible departments for the redistribution of surplus manpower. Gradually, enterprises set up the system of permanent workers who, generally speaking, cannot be dismissed. This system helped stabilize production and employment but had disadvantages reflected in the phrases "everybody eating out of one big pot" and having an "iron rice bowl".

In the 1960s, after the readjustment of the national economy, both production and construction grew rapidly. After reviewing the First-Five-Year Plan, the state came to apply a flexible method to solve the employment problem. For example, the government could provide jobs for people or people could find work by themselves. The government encouraged the development of handicrafts, service trades and the retail industry based on collective ownership in the cities and towns. People also could do temporary work or engage in agriculture and sideline production. Employment service centres were set up which organized and trained the idle labour force.

The "cultural revolution" of 1966 to 1976 brought about serious employment problem. Under the influence of the ultral-left trend, many people in the cities went to the country while many people in the country came to the cities. Within 11 years, the government mobilized 15 million middle-school graduates for settlement in rural areas while more than 13 million peasants came to the cities to work through all kinds of channels. After 1979, great numbers of young people returned to the cities to await employment. Meanwhile, those peasants who had come to the cities stayed on, and the employment problem became serious.

Another factor was the slow development of the national economy coupled with a fast population growth. About 100 million people were born during the 1950s and early 1960s. These people have now reached the age of employment.

The structure of the national economy also contributed to the problems. For many years, undue stress was put on the development of heavy industry. The technically simpler and labour-intensive light industry, commerce and service trades suffered. Further, the structure of ownership blocked many employment channels. Undue stress was laid on the transition of collective ownership to ownership by the whole people, and individual economy was abolished.

Finally, the over-centralized economic management system in which only the state could allocate jobs gave no impetus to local departments and enterprises to solve the employment problem. Job seekers received no encouragement to find their own jobs.

(3) RECENT PROGRESS

Between 1977 and 1980, even when economic conditions were poor, the government managed to arrange employment for 29 million people. With the current drive for modernization and development of economic construction, people will have more chances to get jobs.

The main measures for arranging employment for

young people awaiting jobs from 1977 to 1980 are:

People Newly Employed in Cities and Towns (1977-1980)
(In 10,000 persons)

		1977	1978	1979	1980	Total Number in the Four Years (1977-1980)
	Total number of people employed in cities and towns	520.4	544.4	920.6	900	2,867.4
Main Source of the Newly Employed	People awaiting employment in cities and towns	226.3	159.7	499.5	534	1,419.5
	Middle school graduates back from the countryside	84.0	115.2	189	88.5	476.7
	Rural work force	120.6	148.4	70.8	127.4	467.2
	College, secondary specialized school and secondary technical school graduates	49.9	37.7	33.4	80	201

A New Policy of Employment. Under the new policy, guided by the state over-all plan, the labour departments still provide jobs for people. But people can also organize themselves for jobs or find work by themselves.

Readjusting the Structure of Employment. While readjusting the industrial structure and the structure of ownership, the government has readjusted the structure of employment and opened up ways for employment of the collective and individual economy. Commerce, service trades and consumer goods production will be developed to meet the needs of the people and provide more employment.

In recent years, the government has encouraged the development of various kinds of collective economy. Guided and encouraged by the state over-all plan, the collective economy develops according to the principle that people organize themselves voluntarily and are responsible for their own profits and losses. They distribute earnings according to everyone's work and carry out democratic management. The collective economy engages in the production of articles for daily use, spare parts production, retail, food and drink, repair service, and construction. Since 1979, the collective economy has thrived to play a positive role to develop the economy, make things more convenient for people and create more jobs. These collective economic units have provided jobs for 41 per cent of the young people waiting for employment.

In 1979, the urban individual economy, which is provided for in China's Constitution, also began to develop. Hotels, restaurants, watch and bicycle repair trades and photo studios run by individuals can be found everywhere in the country. Individual working people are recognized and esteemed by the state and society. They and the workers and staff in the state enterprises and the enterprises under collective ownership are to be treated equally without discrimination.

Labour Service Companies. The state has allocated funds to set up labour service companies — some 2,300 throughout the country by 1981 — which perform many duties. Most are set up by labour departments, others by factories, enterprises and institutions. They help develop the collective economy and give aid to people who are looking on their own for jobs. They train and educate young people awaiting employment and introduce them to enterprises for suitable jobs.

Vocational and Technical Training. Every district and enterprise starts technical training for young people awaiting employment, usually middle-school graduates without any technical skills. The training enables them to take an active role in production once hired in enterprises under collective ownership and ownership by the whole people. It also helps them prepare to organize enterprises under collective ownership or to work on their own.

2. WAGE SCALE

(1) WAGES IN NEW CHINA

The old wage system inherited by the government on the founding of the People's Republic in 1949 was semi-colonial, semi-feudal and irrational. In 1952, the government began to reform the old wage system according to the socialist principle of distribution — from each according to his ability, to each according to his work. In 1956, a new unified wage system was set up which forms the basis of the wage system. Over the past two decades, the government has readjusted wages several times and set up a system of bonuses, piece wages and various kinds of job subsidies. The yearly average monetary wage of each person in enterprises under ownership by the whole people was 803 yuan in 1980, an 80 per cent increase over the 446 yuan in 1952 and a yearly average increase of 2.1 per cent. After deducting the rising cost of living expenses, the yearly average wage of workers and staff increased 31.2 per cent over that of 1952, and the yearly average

Number of Workers and Staff and Their Wages in Enterprises Under Ownership by the Whole People

	1952	1957	1965	1975	1979	1980
Number of People at the End of the Year (In 10,000 persons)	1,580	2,451	3,738	6,426	7,693	8,019
Total Wages (In 100 million yuan)	68	156	235	386	529	628
Average Wages (Yuan)	446	637	652	613	705	803
Indexed to 1952	100	142.8	146.2	137.4	158.1	180

Number of Workers and Staff and Their Wages in Enterprises Under Collective Ownership

	1977	1978	1979	1980
Number of People at the End of the Year (In 100,000 persons)	1,916	2,048	2,274	2,425
Total Wages (In 100 million yuan)	89	100.2	117.2	144.6
Average Wages (Yuan)	459	489	542	624

increase was 1 per cent. Over the past two decades, the average wage of workers and staff increased slowly, but the number of employed in cities and towns increased quickly. So the number of family members supported by every employed person has been reduced year by year. With this quick increase in income of family members, living standards have greatly improved compared with that of the initial post-Liberation period.

At present, China has several ways of paying wages. They include time wages, piece wages, bonuses and job subsidies. With time wages, wage standards are fixed according to the technical complexity involved, labour intensity, working conditions and responsibility. Wages are paid by the month, day or hour. Piece wages are calculated according to the number of acceptable products turned out and the predetermined rates per unit. Bonuses are a supplemental form of time wages in which workers

and staff get paid extra if they fulfil their quota with ex-
cellence, efficiency, safety and economy of raw material.
Workers can also get subsidies to compensate for difficult
working conditions such as field work, underground work,
or work under high temperatures.

The Chinese government will make gradual changes
in the current wage system — which was formulated 20
years ago — to suit today's socialist modernization.

(2) WAGE SYSTEM

Time Wages. Most of workers and staff in China get
time wages. Just after Liberation, the wage system
throughout the country was not unified. In the old Liberated Areas, there was a supply system, a part supply
and part wage system, and a system of calculating wages
in kind. In the new Liberated Areas, the wage system left
over from old China was practised. The supply system
was practised only by a few. The current time wage system, formulated after the reform of the wage system in
1956, operates in two ways. The system of professional
wage grades applies to personnel of government organizations, scientific research institutions, educational, public
health and cultural departments, and among technical
and managerial personnel of factories and mines. Workers
in factories and mines are paid according to the workers'
wage grades.

Professional wage grades — there are 24 grades in
the wage scale among administrative personnel of state
organizations. The wages of the highest grade is 12 times
those of the lowest. Among technical personnel, there
are 17 grades. The highest is 9 times that of the lowest.

Scientific, cultural, educational, public health and sports departments have their own wage grades system. The state divides the country into eight zones according to economic levels and living standards. Each zone is separated by a 3 per cent difference in pay.

Workers' wage grades — enterprises pay workers according to a basic system of eight wage grades. In some enterprises, there are only seven or six grades. The highest wage is about three times that of the lowest. The wages of each grade vary in different areas and trades.

Oil Drillers' Wages in Different Areas

Area	Monthly Pay of the First Wage Grade and the Eighth Wage Grade (Yuan)	Ratio Between the Highest and Lowest Wages
Heilongjiang Province	35.5 — 113.6	3.2 : 1
Sichuan Province	32 — 102.4	3.2 : 1
Yumen, Gansu Province	44 — 140.8	3.2 : 1
Xinjiang Uygur Autonomous Region	45.1 — 144.32	3.2 : 1
Qinghai Province	44 — 141	3.2 : 1

Industrial Workers' Wages of Different Trades

Trade	Monthly Pay of the First Wage Grade and the Eighth Wage Grade (Yuan)	Ratio Between the Highest and Lower Wages
Coal mining in Liaoning Province	34 — 107.1	3.15 : 1
Oil extraction in Liaoning and Jilin provinces	34 — 103.7	3.05 : 1
Paper-making factories in Jilin Province	31 — 88.35	2.85 : 1
Textile factories in Northeast China	31.5 — 85	2.7 : 1
Cigarette factories in Liaoning Province	28.5 — 71.25	2.5 : 1

Note: The textile industry has a wage scale of 15 grades, the highest being the 15th.

Depending on the national economy and productivity, the state promotes workers and staff within a certain period of time, usually according to their own wage scales. In some cases, both the minimum and maximum norms in wage raises are prescribed. Promotions are decided according to workers' attitude towards work, ability, contributions and seniority. From 1956 (the year when the national wage system was reformed) to 1980, there were seven promotions in 1959, 1961, 1963, 1971, 1977, 1978 and 1979.

Piece Wages and Bonuses. The system of bonuses is now applied throughout China. The system of piece wages is practised in some enterprises. Both forms reflect the principle of distribution according to work. The percentage of workers getting piece wages in state enterprises varied depending on whether the principle of distribution according to work was applied or not. In 1952, workers getting piece wages accounted for 32.5 per cent of the total number of workers; in 1960 they accounted for 5 per cent; in 1963 they accounted for 19.9 per cent. From 1966 to 1976, the state basically stopped piece wages. Bonuses also were sometimes not given during these years. During the First Five-Year Plan period, there were bonuses for overfulfilling production quota, economizing on raw materials, producing high quality products or creating new products. During the Second Five-Year Plan period, bonuses for all these were changed into comprehensive bonuses. From 1967 to 1975, bonuses and pay for overfulfilling production quota were changed into additional wages which were given to workers monthly.

After 1976, the state gradually resumed practice of piece wages and bonuses to carry out the principle of distribution according to work. In April 1980, the State Planning Commission, State Economic Commission and State Bureau of Labour jointly issued "Temporary Provisions for Piece Wages in State Enterprises". It stipulates that the piece wage system can be practised among the workers in enterprises where it is appropriate. The two forms of piece wages include one for individual piece-work and another for collective piecework. At present, excess piece wages are limited to 30 per cent of the total sum of wages.

In May 1978, the State Council issued the "Circular for Practising the System of Bonuses and Piece Wages". Bonuses come in general from the total sum of workers' wages, do not exceed 10-12 per cent of it and are included in the production costs. From 1979, the state decided to experiment in extending some state enterprises' rights to autonomy as a way of changing the system of economic management. The bonuses of the workers and staff in these enterprises are taken out of the part of profits that is reserved for the enterprises. Workers and staff gener-ally get bonuses monthly or quarterly, and occasionally at the end of the year. After fulfilling every aspect of the state plan, the enterprises decide their own standards on the bonuses, which generally equal one and a half months' or two months' average wages. In a few enter-prises that have achieved great outstanding success, the bonuses may equal a maximum of three months' average wages.

Job Subsidies. The state has instituted a system of job subsidies for workers and staff who work under spe-cial conditions and in remote border districts. There are four categories of job subsidies. They are: 1) district job subsidies which encourage people to go to remote border districts or districts where conditions are hard; 2) job subsidies for ensuring health; 3) job subsidies for compen-sating for extra exertions in work; 4) job subsidies for guaranteeing the real wages of workers and staff. At present there are several kinds of job subsidies (such as those for work on islands, in remote border districts, forest regions, for field work, underground work, work on metorological observatory stations where conditions are hard, construction work, or work under high temperatures). Besides, there are ship crew's food subsidies, subsidies for motor-vehicle drivers, train crew, postal and telecommunication workers doing field work, leaders of work teams in factories, teachers doing extra teaching, and sports subsidies and subsidies for outstanding sports men and women.

To meet the needs of socialist modernization, the income of the workers and staff will be increased gradually and the wage system and the system of economic management will be reformed in co-ordination with the development of production and rise of labour productivity.

3. PEOPLE'S INCOME AND SPENDING

Since the founding of the People's Republic, the standards of income and spending have gone up as industry and agriculture have developed. During the initial period of Liberation (1949-1952) and the First Five-Year Plan period (1953-1957), the standards of income and spending rose quickly with the recovery of the national economy.   Later, living standards rose slowly because from 1958 to 1965, the state paid great attention to accumulation and less attention to people's consumption. The 10 years of the "cultural revolution", brought great damage to China's national economy.   After 1976, the government has done much to improve the standard of living. Within four years (from 1977 to 1980), income and spending in cities and rural areas rose quickly again. The changes experienced in this area since the founding of People's Republic are as follows:

(1) PEOPLE'S INCOME

People's Income in Cities and Towns. In the fourth quarter of 1980, the state statistical departments made a survey of about 8,000 families of workers and staff in 44 big, medium and small cities. In 1980, the average monthly per capita income was 42.8 yuan, a 111 per cent increase over the 20.29 yuan of 1964. The yearly average increase was 4.8 per cent. During this time, prices for food, rent, water and electricity, and public transportation remained basically stable. Taking into consideration the prices of some commodities which had gone up, the real income of workers and staff increased by an average of 3.3 per cent a year. The wages of workers and staff increased several times during this period, especially in 1977 and 1979 when about 40 per cent of all the workers and staff in the country got raises in pay. The government also worked to arrange employment for people, and the number of employed in each family increased. According to the survey in 1980, the average number of employed in a family was 2.35 people in 1980, as compared with 1.56 people in 1964. Thus, the number of family members supported by each employed (including the employed himself) was reduced from 3.4 members in 1964 to 1.83 members in 1980. As a result of family planning, the size of the family had become smaller. Families which had thus relatively increased their income made up 35 per cent of the total. Workers and staff received an average of 400-500 yuan each year in benefits in the form of labour insurance, free medical care, bonuses and allowances.

Statistics show that the number of families with higher incomes increased while those with lower income de-

creased.   The number of low-income families with an
average monthly income per person dropped from 32 per

Size and Income of Families

	1964	The Fourth Quarter of 1980
Average number of persons in a family	5.3	4.3
Average number of employed in a family	1.56	2.35
Average number of people supported by each wage-earner (himself included)	3.4	1.83
Average monthly income per person	20.29 yuan	42.8 yuan

Note: The data are drawn from different fields, so a true
comparison cannot be made.

The 1964 data is based on a survey of 3,573 households of
workers and staff who are employed by state-owned industrial
enterprises, commercial establishments, cultural and education
departments, government and mass organizations in 40 large,
medium and small cities.   The data of the fourth quarter of 1980
is based on a survey of 7,962 households of workers and staff
in both state and collective owned enterprises and institutions,
including industry, capital construction, agriculture and forestry,
transportation, post and telecommunications, commerce, urban
public, utilities, science, culture, education, public health
finance and government and mass organizations in 44 large,
medium and small cities.

cent of the total in 1964 to 1 per cent in the fourth quarter of 1980, while families with an average monthly income of over 50 yuan per person increased from 1.3 per cent of the total in 1964 to 14.2 per cent in 1980.

Rural Income. In 31 years, Chinese peasants' income has grown remarkably. The Land Reform immediately after Liberation freed landless or land-poor peasants from exorbitant rents, which amounted to 35 million tons of grain paid to the landlords every year. But after 1957, agriculture developed slowly under the erroneous idea of stressing grain production while ignoring a diversified economy and household sideline production. In 1976, the average net annual income of each household from both collective production and individual sideline production was 113 yuan, only 40 yuan more than that in 1957. This means an average yearly increase of two yuan over that period. In 1978, the state readjusted some of its rural economic policies and greatly raised the purchasing prices of farm produce and sideline products. Since then the peasants' income has increased considerably. The average net income of each peasant in 1980 was 74 yuan more than in 1977. The amount of the increased income in the three years from 1978 to 1980 was much higher than the total amount of increase in the previous 19 years. In 1978, 31 per cent of families were low-income ones with an average yearly net income of under 100 yuan per member. In 1980 that proportion had dropped to 9.8 per cent. The proportion of well-off families in which each member's yearly average net income was above 300 yuan increased from 4.8 to 11.1 per cent in the same period.

With the higher incomes of people in cities and rural areas, holdings of ready money and bank deposits have grown visibly. The average bank deposit per person throughout the country went from 13.9 yuan in 1957 to 82 yuan in 1980, an increase of 5.9 times. From 1977 to 1980 the average savings deposit per person went up by 36 yuan.

Consumption Levels

Year	Per Capita Consumption Levels (On the given year's prices in yuan)			Index Figures in Constant Prices (1952 = 100)		
	For the Whole Country	Peasants	Others	For the Whole Country	Peasants	Others
1952	76	62	148	100	100	100
1957	102	79	205	122.9	117.1	126.3
1965	125	100	237	126.4	116	136.5
1975	158	124	324	156.9	143.1	181.1
1978	175	132	383	171.3	151.3	205.9
1980	224	168	477	199	172.8	234.4

Note: Figures in this table are calculated on the basis of the total individual consumption within the total expenditure of national income and on the basis of average population figures.

(2) CONSUMPTION

Higher Consumption.   With higher incomes, living standards have improved. The average level of material consumption in 1980 was 224 yuan per person throughout

Pattern of Consumption

	Pattern of Consumption of Urban Dwellers (%)			Pattern of Consumption of Peasants (%)	
	1964	1980		1964	1980
Total Living Expenditure	100	100	Total Living Expenditure	100	100
Food	59.2	56	Food	67.1	61.8
Clothing	11	17.2	Clothing	9.2	12.3
Articles for use	10.9	16.8	Articles for use	7.7	9.4
Housing	4.4	2.2	Housing	3.4	7.9
Fuel	4.3	2.4	Fuel	9.9	6
Culture and Service	10.2	5.4	Culture and Service	2.7	2.6

the country. The figure for peasants was 168 yuan and
that for everyone else 477 yuan. Allowing for price increase, this was 99 per cent higher than in 1952, a yearly
average increase of 2.5 per cent, or 2 per cent for peasants
and 3 per cent for others. In the four years from 1977 to
1980, the average annual increase was 5.6 per cent, a much
higher increase than the 2 per cent in the 24 years from
1953 to 1976. This is shown below:

Changing Pattern of Consumption. With rising consumption in town and country, the pattern of consumption has changed. In the early period of Liberation, people had much lower income and had to support more people. They spent their money first on food and clothing
and then on daily necessities. With higher income, especially in recent years, more money is being spent on
clothing and other articles. According to investigations
into the income and expenditure of rural and urban families, the proportion of income spent on food dropped while
the proportion spent on clothing and other articles rose
between 1964 and 1980.

(3) HIGHER CONSUMPTION OF MAIN CONSUMER GOODS.

With the increase in income, the types of food, clothes
and other goods that people purchase also have changed.
The consumption of high-quality food, clothes and durable
goods grew by a big margin. The amount of meat, poultry
and eggs sold is increasing faster than that of grain and
other staples. Within the staples, the volume of wheat
flour and rice has increased while that of coarse grain has
gone down. Both the quantity and quality of clothes have
gone up. In the 1950s, cotton was the main textile worn by

the Chinese people. Since the 1970s, cotton gradually
has been giving way to synthetic fibres, wool, silks and
satins. In other consumer goods the tendency is towards
high-quality durables. The proportion of bicycles, watches, sewing machines, radios and televisions in the total
retail sales of consumer goods reached from 0.5 per cent
in 1952 to 24.5 per cent in 1980. In recent years, people
in the cities have begun to buy washing machines, refrig-
erators, electric fans, recorders, cameras, furniture and
cosmetics. High-quality bicycles, watches, sewing machines and radios are highly prized by consumers in rural
areas.

Durable Goods Owned Per 100 Persons in 1980

	In Units of 10,000	Number of Units per 100 Persons		
		Total	Urban	Rural
Sewing Machine	4,604	4.7	11.2	3.2
Bicycle	9,619	9.7	27.9	5.6
Watch	12,765	12.9	44.4	5.8
Radio	11,910	12.1	29.6	8.1
TV	902	0.9	3.5	0.2

Family Life of Workers and Staff Members. According to a survey of nearly 8,000 households of workers and staff members in 44 cities in the fourth quarter of 1980, the monthly consumption of grain was 13.05 kg. per head — an increase of 3.2 per cent over 1964; edible vegetable oil, 0.335 kg.; fish and shrimp, 0.655 kg.; eggs, 0.29 kg.; sugar, 0.23 kg.; and vegetables, 19.45 kg. — an increase of from 68 to 81 per cent over 1964; pork, beef and mutton, 1.56 kg.; poultry, 0.15 kg.; wine, 0.255 kg.; candy, 0.11 kg.; and pastry, 0.255 kg.— an increase of from 50 to 280 per cent over 1964. As for clothing, every 100 persons each month bought 53 metres of cotton cloth and man-made fibre, a 51 per cent increase over 1964; 1.45 kg. of knitting wool and woollen knitwear; 2.3 metres of woollen cloth; 1.3 pieces of woollen clothes; 4.4 metres of silk and satin; 5.1 pairs of leather shoes — an increase of from 100 to 480 per cent over 1964. By the end of 1980, every 100 households had an average of 127 bicycles, 66 sewing machines, 224 watches, 85 radios, 32 televisions, 5.4 recorders, and 22 electric fans.

Family Life in Rural Areas. According to a survey of more than 15,900 peasant households in 1980, the average annual expenditure was 162 yuan per person, an increase of 70 per cent over the 95 yuan in 1965 and 21 per cent over the 135 yuan in 1979. In the consumption of grain, the proportion of wheat flour and rice reached from 54 per cent in 1979 to 63 per cent in 1980. The consumption of edible oil was 2.5 kg.; pork, 7.75 kg.; and sugar, 1.05 kg. In addition, the consumption of eggs, fish, shrimp and wine also increased a great deal. As for clothing, the average annual consumption of cotton cloth was 5.2 metres for each person, an in-

crease of 40 per cent over that of 1964. Consumption
of man-made fibres, wool, woollen cloth, and rubber
shoes increased several times. Durable goods such as
bicycles, sewing machines, watches, and radios were also
sold much faster in rural areas than previous years.

The cash income of peasants also increased and their
purchasing power grew. The proportion of expenditure
on commodities in the total consumption of the peasants
increased from 40 per cent in 1978 to 50.4 per cent in
1980 and that of self-sufficient consumption decreased
from 60.2 per cent to 49.6 per cent during the same
period.

In recent years, thanks to increase of income,
peasants have built more houses. The new houses built
in the three years between 1978 and 1980 totalled 900
million square metres in floor space. By the end of 1980,
each person in the rural area had 11.6 square metres of
floor space, nine of which are living space.

Despite these advances, the level of consumption of
the Chinese people is still lower than that of the developed countries. Money spent on food is higher than on
high-quality consumer goods, and household electrical
appliances are not in wide use. Generally speaking, the
improvement in living standard was slow for a long
period in the past because of the stress laid under
"Leftist" thinking on high speed and more accumulation,
on "production first and standard of living second". The
fast population growth also contributed to sluggish
growth in consumption level.

In recent years, the consumption level of peasants
grew faster than that of the workers and staff members,
narrowing the gap in living standard between workers
and peasants. But generally speaking the living standard

in rural areas is comparitively low. There is still a great disparity between workers and peasants in such things as food, clothing, fuel, daily necessities, recreation and medical service. Because of different natural conditions, rich and poor areas still exist. The gap between workers and peasants has not narrowed more over the years because of low productivity in agriculture and its slower growth compared to that of industry. The average output value of each man power in agriculture is only around 400 yuan annually or 1,100 kilogrammes of grain.

4. LABOUR INSURANCE AND WELFARE

(1) GENERAL ACCOUNT

After the founding of New China in 1949, as production developed, China gradually established a labour insurance system, which ensures income and material aid for retired, ill, injured or disabled workers and staff members. In 1951, the Labour Insurance Regulations were instituted among the workers and staff members of some industries; in 1953, they were amended to raise the standard of benefits and their scope of application was extended. Since then, Chinese workers and staff members have not needed to worry about their livelihood when they give birth, retire, die or become injured, ill or disabled.

State-owned enterprises also take care of their employees in other ways. They have built large numbers of residential buildings and hospitals and run welfare services such as dining halls, nurseries and kindergartens. Together the Labour Insurance Regulations and this welfare system promote production by protecting the health and ensuring the basic living standards of workers and staff members.

Workers and staff members in state enterprises, institutions and organs need not hand in any money to finance the labour insurance and welfare. The necessary funds are furnished by the state, and allotments for labour insurance and welfare have steadily increased. In 1952, for example, the state allocated a sum equal to 14 per cent of the total payroll of workers and staff members to labour insurance and welfare funds while in 1980 the funds equalled 18.4 per cent of the year's total payroll, and with the addition of various allowances, benefits and money spent on other collective welfare, this sum reached 80 per cent of the total payroll.

(2) LABOUR INSURANCE

Labour Insurance System. Labour insurance at present is provided according to two systems. One benefits the workers and staff members of state-owned enterprises while the other applies to the workers and staff members of state organs, institutions and people's organizations.

The former labour insurance system is carried out according to the Labour Insurance Regulations of the People's Republic of China which were first promulgated by the Government Administrative Council on February 26, 1951, and then amended in 1953. The amended version raised the level of pensions for retired workers and those disabled by work accidents and raised benefits for sick leave and allowance for the lineal dependents of a deceased worker. Since 1956 the scope of benefits has greatly expanded. From 1958 to 1978 some amendments and additions were made in the provisions concerning retirement and medical care.

The latter labour insurance system is carried out according to separate regulations which have been promulgated by the Chinese government since 1952. These regulations, having undergone amendments and additions, form the basis of the labour insurance system for the workers and staff members in the state organs, institutions and people's organizations. On the whole, the standard of benefits in the two systems is equivalent, although the specific details of benefits differ. For instance, workers in state organs and institutions receive higher benefits in case of sick leave and death than do workers in state enterprises; however, the former are not entitled to medical allowances for their lineal dependents while the latter are.

General Characteristics of the Chinese Labour Insurance System. In short, the Chinese labour insurance system has the following characteristics:

1) All workers and staff members employed in state enterprises, institutions and organs are equally entitled to the benefits of labour insurance, regardless of their race, sex, age or nationality.

2) All the expenses for labour insurance are borne by the state or local units which employ the workers and staff members.

3) Benefits under different provisions are linked with one another. For instance, a worker or a staff member who falls sick can enjoy free medical care and other benefits as stipulated for the case of sick leave. If he fails to be cured and is considered disabled, the state will offer him the benefits for the disabled.

4) The state takes fully responsibility for the workers and staff members. There is no time limit for benefits. For instance, every worker or staff member who falls sick enjoys the benefits for sick leave and medical care until he recovers, dies or his sickness is diagnosed as a disability.

Concrete Benefits of Labour Insurance. Although the concrete benefits of labour insurance are stipulated in separate regulations for enterprises and for organs, institutions and people's organizations, for convenience of comparison they can be described here together:

1) Childbirth benefits. Pregnant workers and staff members enjoy free medical care, including pre-natal examinations, hospitalization and child delivery, and receive a birth allowance from their enterprises. In addition they are entitled to a total of 56 days maternity leave. During this period they receive their full wages. Recent family planning policies also provide an only-child allowance for families that pledge to have only one child. The mother of an only child receives a more extended fully paid maternity leave.

2) Sick benefits. For each medical service, workers or staff members pay only a 10-cent registration fee; all the medical expenses they incur, including diagnosis, medical treatment, examination, surgery, medicine and hospitalization, are paid by the state. During a period of sick leave which is less than six months, those who are employed in state enterprises receive from 40 to 100 per cent of their wages, depending on their length of employment. When their sick leave exceeds six months they receive from 40 to 60 per cent of their wages or 40 per cent of the average wage of their enterprise, which

ever is higher. They enjoy this benefit until they re-
cover and return to work, become officially disabled or
die. As for those employed in state organs or institutions, they receive full wages during their first two
months of sick leave, from 90 to 100 per cent of their
wages from the third month on and from 70 to 100 per
cent of their wages from the seventh month on, all the
percentages also decided by the length of their working
years.

3) Benefits for injury. If workers or staff members employed in state enterprises get injured while at
work, their medical expenses and two-thirds of their
board expenses for hospitalization are paid by the state.
During their sick leave, full wages are paid to them as
usual. If the injury does not occur during working
hours, the benefits equal those mentioned in the case
of sickness.

4) Disability benefits. Workers or staff members
of enterprises who have become disabled by an on-the-
job accident are transferred to a post which requires
less physical strength. If the transfer causes a reduction
of their wages, they receive, as compensation, another
amount, from 10 to 30 per cent of their wages, depending on the amount of reduction. Workers or staff members who are employed in state enterprises, organs or
institutions who become completely disabled by an on-
the-job accident can retire. Their retirement pension is
paid according to their circumstances. If they need an
attendant to help them they receive 90 per cent of their
monthly wage or 35 yuan a month, whichever is higher.
In addition they receive monthly nursing expenses. If
they do not need an attendant they receive 80 percent
of their monthly wage or 35 yuan a month, whichever

is higher, until they die. If workers or staff members become completely disabled by serious illness or by an off-the-job accident, they can stay at home and receive 40 per cent of their monthly wage or 20 yuan, whichever is higher. If the desablement occurs at the age of 50 or later for men or 45 or later for women, they are entitled. to enjoy retirement benefits, which are much higher than the foregoing.

5) Retirement benefits. In state enterprises, organs and institutions, male workers and staff members retire at the age of 60, female staff members at 55 and female workers at 50, if they have already worked for 10 or more years. Those who work under conditions of high temperature or in mine pits or other conditions hazardous to health are entitled to retire five years earlier. Their retirement pension is paid according to the length of their working years, from 60 to 70 per cent of their wages or 25 yuan, whichever is higher. Those participated in the revolution before the founding of the People's Republic of China, or are national model workers and combat heroes enjoy higher benefits.

6) Death benefits. The enterprises and state are responsible for the workers and employees' funeral expense and pay an allowance to the lineal dependents of the deceased. If workers and employees of enterprises die from work accidents, their funeral expense, equal to three months' average wage at their enterprise, will be paid. Also, from 25 to 50 per cent of their wage, depending on the number of lineal dependents supported by the deceased, will be given to their families every month. If they die from causes other than work accidents, their funeral expense can equal two months' average wage at their enterprise. In addition, their lineal dependents

receive, just once as relief money, six to 12 months' wage of the deceased, depending on the number of lineal dependents. If the workers or staff members employed in state organs or institutions die, their families will receive a one-time payment of 200 to 300 yuan as funeral expense and 400 to 700 yuan, decided by the rank of the deceased and the cause of death, as the allowance for the lineal dependents of the deceased. If the lineal dependents meet with difficulties in supporting themselves, an allowance is given to them regularly or incidentally according to their situation.

7) Insurance benefits for the lineal dependents of workers and staff members in state enterprises. Enterprises are held responsible for half of the medical and surgical expenses incurred by lineal dependents. The allowance for their funeral expense equals one-third to one-half of the monthly average wage of the enterprises.

(3) WELFARE BENEFITS OF WORKERS AND STAFF MEMBERS

Welfare benefits of workers and staff members consist of three components: housing; welfare facilities such as hospitals, nurseries, sanatoriums and dining halls; and welfare allowances and subsidies.

Housing. Since the founding of New China in 1949, China has invested 53,400 million yuan to build residential buildings of 677 million square metres of floor space for over 13.5 million households in cities, towns and industrial and mining areas. In 1952, 7.51 million square metres of residential floor space were completed, while during the period of the First Five-Year Plan (1953-57) the newly constructed floor space covered 94.54 million square metres. In addition, a large number of houses were built by workers and staff members with the aid of their units. During the period from 1978 to 1980, China built residential buildings with a total of 180 million square metres of floor space, benefiting 3.6 million households in cities and towns. In 1980 alone, China invested 10,800 million yuan to build residential buildings of 82.3 million square metres of floor space for 1,640,000 households. Despite the achievements of the last three years, the Chinese inhabitants of towns and cities still have a limited area to live in — about 3.9 square metres per person.

Investment in Housing and Completed Floor Space

Year	Investment in million of yuan	Floor space in million of square metres
1953-57	5,013	945.4
1958-62	4,866	1,101.2
1963-65	2,787	427.1
1976-79	15,820	1,525.6
1980	10,700	823

Note: These statistics cover units owned by the whole people.

Most of the residential buildings constructed in the 1950s and 1960s had three or four floors while those completed in recent years generally have five or six floors. A number of the residences in large and medium-sized cities have even more stories. As part of the construction, conveyance systems are completed for gas, water, electricity and plumbing, and so are roads, public buildings, schools, kindergartens, shops, post offices, grain shops, and so on.

Rents in China differ from place to place and from unit to unit, but in general they are quite low. In Beijing, for instance, a flat of two rooms with a total of 25 square metres of floor space rents for 3.5 yuan per month, which only amounts to 3 per cent of the average monthly income of a family.

Welfare Facilities. All Chinese workers and staff members enjoy free medical care and the lineal dependents of those employed in enterprises enjoy partially free medical care. In 1953, there were altogether 1,345 hospitals with 121,000 beds and 270 convalescent hospitals and homes in Chinese cities. During the First Five-Year Plan period, such facilities grew rapidly. By 1957, there were 1,656 city hospitals with 221,000 beds and 835 convalescent hospitals and homes. Since 1976, such facilities have developed even faster: in 1980 alone, city hospitals increased to 5,876 with 768,000 beds.

For the convenience of workers and staff members, Chinese enterprises, organs and institutions have all set up dining halls, kindergartens, nurseries, libraries, clubs and other facilities. In addition the state subsidizes the dining halls, so that workers and staff members need not spend much money for food. Chinese kindergartens and nurseries consist of two kinds: one kind is run by the state-owned units such as educational departments, enterprises, organs and institutions; the other kind is run by neighbourhood committees. As both kinds receive state subsidies, the nursery fees and food expenses of kindergartens and nurseries can be kept low, thus lightening the financial burden of workers and staff members. In 1957 there were altogether 16,400 nurseries while by 1980, the number of nurseries had increased to 170,000 enrolling a total of 11,507,700 children.

Moreover, enterprises and institutions often set up libraries, reading rooms and clubs to provide cultural and recreational activities for workers and staff members.

Welfare Allowances and Subsidies. Many Chinese workers and staff members enjoy various welfare allowances, the principal ones of which are: allowances for severely cold regions, for room heating in winter, for transportation fees in cities which have a population of 500,000 or more, for travel fees to visit close relatives and for those who have financial difficulties.

In order to solve the problem of long-distance delivery of agricultural products and non-staple food to factories, mining enterprises, state organs and army units that are located far from towns and cities, the state supports units that are suited to develop agricultural and non-staple food production. In 1980, factories and mining enterprises cultivated a total of seven million mu[1] of land, which yielded 500,000 tons of grain, 1,500,000 tons of vegetables, and large quantities of oil-bearing crops, meat, fruit, and so on, improving the life of the workers and staff members there to some extent.

----

[1] A mu is equivalent to 1/15 hectare or approximately 1/6 acre.

In addition, the Chinese government pays workers and staff members a large amount of grain and edible oil allowances, the sum in 1980 alone exceeding 10,000 million yuan.

5. LABOUR PROTECTION

Since soon after the founding of New China, the Chinese government has paid much attention to labour protection, formulating and promulgating labour protection policies and regulations. Meanwhile every year the state allocates a labour protection fund to improve working conditions. To strengthen labour insurance, factories and mining enterprises adopt effective safety measures in production, work out their own labour protection regulations and supervise the implementation of all the regulations, thus ensuring their employees' safety and health.

(1) REGULATIONS AND MEASURES OF LABOUR PROTECTION

Labour Protection Laws and Regulations. During the period of the First Five-Year Plan (1953-1957) the state promulgated 15 kinds of laws and regulations, including *Regulations on Factory Safety and Sanitation*, *Regulations Concerning Safe Working on Construction Work* and *Regulations Governing Reports on Casualties and Accidents Resulting in Injury or Death to Workers and Staff Members*. Adding in the regulations formulated by the central departments and local organizations, there were before 1979 altogether 300 kinds. The implementation of these laws and regulations plays an important role in improving working conditions, strengthening the management of labour protection, preventing accidents and promoting production in enterprises.

In 1979, the state reaffirmed the laws and regulations that had been proved effective in practice and began to institute new ones, such as the *Laws on Mine Safety and Sanitation, Regulations on Mine Safety and Sanitation Control,* a draft *Standards of Noise Sanitation for Industrial Enterprises* and *Regulations on Women's Labour Protection.*

Measures of Labour Protection. In order to carry out the labour protection policies and regulations effectively, the government departments in charge of labour and enterprises take the following measures:

1. Establishing labour protection organs at all levels, propagating labour protection and training labour protection cadres. Since 1949, labour departments, the departments in charge of production and trade unions at all levels have established managing organs of labour protection. The State Council founded the Ministry of Labour (now renamed the State Bureau of Labour) while local authorities in different parts of China established their departments in charge of labour, responsible for comprehensive management and supervision. Their concrete tasks are to work out laws and regulations, establish supervisory system, organize safety inspection, supervise and urge enterprises to plan the improvement of working conditions, investigate and compile statistics of accidents and promote scientific research, propaganda and education concerning labour protection. In 1980 the State Bureau of Labour conducted a training course five

times for a total of 500 cadres working in labour protection, compiled teaching materials of more than one million words, published a number of reference books on
labour protection and made several films on safety production. The labour departments of various regions and
units utilize wire broadcasts, pictures, slide shows, films
and live performances to propagate labour protection
among workers and staff members.

From factory level to the workshop level, mines and
enterprises have established labour protection organs
and appointed safety inspectors who are not released
from their own work. The leaders of an enterprise are
responsible for both production and safety. A production plan of an enterprise usually includes safety measures for production. Besides the national and local
trade unions, those at specific mines and enterprises have
also established corresponding organizations to supervise
and inspect the labour protection work.

2) Establishing scientific research and educational
organs. In order to strengthen scientific research on
labour protection and train specialists for this work, the
state labour departments set up the Research Institute
of Labour Protection in 1957 (now the institute is under
the jurisdiction of the Beijing Municipality). Some universities and colleges offer courses of safety and labour
protection techniques for science and engineering students. The Beijing Institute of Labour (now the Beijing
Institute of Economics) has a Department of Labour
Protection. In recent years the state has established 11
research institutes of labour protection in different parts
of China to meet the needs of development of production.
Their technicians often go to factories and mining enterprises to study and manufacture labour protection

devices and instruments, such as anti-explosion devices, dust removers and noise prevention instruments.

3) Striving to improve working conditions. The Constitution of the People's Republic of China stipulates the work hours for workers and staff members and special provisions protecting the special interests of young workers and women workers and staff members. In Chinese enterprises, women workers and staff members enjoy special protection. Pregnant women are offered work suitable for their health condition. In enterprises, nursing rooms are set up for the convenience of women workers and staff members.

Every year the state allocates labour protection funds to industrial departments for the improvement of working conditions. During the First Five-Year Plan it allocated 490 million yuan to solve many serious problems of safety equipment technology and industrial sanitation, including ventilation and drainage in mines, heatstroke prevention and temperature lowering for those who work in hot areas, protection against poisonous gas and silicious dust, reducing the strain of labour and safe operation of electrical instruments. In 1979 the state further stipulated that enterprises should spend 10 to 20 per cent of their funds earmarked for the renewal of fixed assets and technical equipment to improve working conditions. In 1980, despite financial difficulties, the state still allocated funds for the improvement of working conditions.

4) Developing safe production. In order to remove hidden perils in production, factories and mining enterprises mobilize the masses to make extensive checks several times a year. In enterprises safe-production teams are formed to organize workers to participate

in the management of daily safety, carry out and organize the checks and advise the research activities on
safe production, thus perfecting safety facilities all the
time, improving working conditions and maintaining
the safety and health of workers. In 1980, about a dozen
units headed by the State Economic Commission observed a special "Safety Month" publicly on radio and tele-
vision.

(2) SOME ACHIEVEMENTS IN LABOUR PROTECTION

Thank to the great care taken by the Chinese government and the great efforts of enterprises, labour
protection measures have achieved good results in the
mine pits, in loading and transportation, in working conditions high above the ground and at worksites
with high temperatures or much dust.

Safety Equipment Installed in Mine Pits. Before
Liberation, unsafe working conditions and overlong
working hours were the rule. As a result, work-related
illnesses spread and accidents resulting in injury or
death happened frequently. Since Liberation, things
have greatly improved. Labour safety devices are generally installed in mine pits, and mechanization of
mining has been realized step by step. In coal mines,
for instance, mechanization of mining and transportation is replacing dangerous hand mining and human
transportation. Before Liberation, only 30 per cent of
China's mines used mechanical ventilation, so that each
miner could breathe only one cubic metre of fresh air
per minute but now nearly every mine has mechanical

ventilation devices, so that each miner can breathe more than four cubic metres of fresh air per minute. Illumination in the mines has also improved, and effective measures have been adopted in drainage, fire prevention, gas examination and extraction. Zhangjialing Coal Mine in Shaodong County, Hunan Province, for instance, as a super gas mine pit, has become model coal mine in China for its safe and successful extraction of coal. Since 1960 no accidents resulting in severe injury or death have taken place there, and even the number of those resulting in minor injury has decreased year by year.

Protection Against Dusty Harm. In Chinese mines and enterprises outstanding achievements have been made in protection against silicious dust. The state demands that all enterprises that are threatened by silicious dust harm take measures to minimizing silicious dusts in the air to the allowed maximum level of less than 2 mg. per cubic metre. The state also forbids dry drilling and open and dry production. Mining, tunnel construction, geological prospecting and quarrying all take anti-dust measures, such as wet drilling, strengthening ventilation and sprinkling. Machine-parts casting, quartz-powder processing and the smashing, riddling and mixture of raw materials for making glass, porcelain and refractory and the moulding of them are done by wet operation or with ventilation or under airtight and dust free conditions.

Many enterprises dealing with dusts have reduced the density of silicious dust to the state-required standards while some enterprises have achieved even safer levels. In Xialong Tungsten Mine in Jiangxi Prov-

ince, for instance, though silicon dioxide makes up
58 to 97 per cent of the ore, the density of silicious dust
in the air of the mine has reached the state requirement.
From 1958 on, the workers and staff members have had
their lungs X-rayed each year, and none has been found
to be suffering from silicosis even after 22 years working in the mine. All factories and mining enterprises
supply workers and staff members dealing with silicious
dust with protective equipment and special food for the
maintenance of their health. In addition, the industrial
departments, factories and mining enterprises have
established special medical organizations and sanatoriums
at scenic spots with favourable climates in order to cure
their workers who do suffer from silicosis.

**Safety Devices for Loading and Transportation and
Working Under High Temperature or High Above the
Ground.** In old China there were few safety devices
installed for loading and transportation or for working
under high temperature or high above the ground. But
now things have changed completely.

High temperatures in textile mills, machine plants
and smelteries were a serious problem in old China, but
now water and wind cooling equipment is installed in all
textile workshops while in iron and steel works and
machinery and electric industrial enterprises, sprinkling
fans are installed to shower the dry and hot air in addition to ordinary mechanical ventilation. Some enterprises
have even instituted remote operation. In summer, free
cold drinks are supplied to workers and staff members
in smelteries or other high-temperature worksites. The
state has also established special management organs to
supervise and examine, according to safety principles, the

design, manufacture, installation, use and repair of special equipment, such as boilers and pressure-vessels.

Loading and transportation at China's ports has been partly or fully mechanized, thus reducing the burden on dock workers.

Since 1949, China's labour protection has achieved outstanding results, although some health and safety problems remain. For instance, some enterprises do not manage properly or neglect education in safety measures. Seventy per cent of all work accidents that have occurred were a result of mistaken orders or operation against rules.

To make the labour protection suit the needs of socialist modernization, Chinese labour departments and factories and mining enterprises are trying hard to develop technical training, strengthen safety and protection measures in production and improve management and legislation so as to safeguard workers' and staff members' health and well being even more.

社 会 生 活

《中国手册》编辑委员会编

✹

外文出版社出版
（中国北京百万庄路24号）
外文印刷厂印刷
中国国际图书贸易总公司
（中国国际书店）发行
北京399信箱
1985年（32开）第一版
编号：（英）17050—199

00265
17—E—1669P